okashi

sweet treats made with love

okashi

sweet treats made with love

keiko ishida

Marshall Cavendish
Cuisine

Designer: Bernard Go Kwang Meng

Photographer: Kiyoshi Yoshizawa, Jambu Studio

Published by Marshall Cavendish Cuisine
An imprint of Marshall Cavendish International

Other Marshall Cavendish Offices:
Marshall Cavendish Corporation. 99 White Plains Road, Tarrytown NY 10591-9001, USA • Marshall Cavendish International (Thailand) Co Ltd. 253 Asoke, 12th Flr, Sukhumvit 21 Road, Klongtoey Nua, Wattana, Bangkok 10110, Thailand • Marshall Cavendish (Malaysia) Sdn Bhd, Times Subang, Lot 46, Subang Hi-Tech Industrial Park, Batu Tiga, 40000 Shah Alam, Selangor Darul Ehsan, Malaysia

National Library Board Singapore Cataloguing in Publication Data
Ishida, Keiko, 1965-
Okashi : sweet treats made with love / Keiko Ishida. – Singapore : Marshall Cavendish Cuisine, c2009.
p. cm.
ISBN-13 : 978-981-261-780-4

1. Desserts – Japan. 2. Cookery, Japanese. I. Title.

TX773
641.860952 — dc22   OCN320282118

Printed in Singapore by Craft Print International Ltd

contents

Dedication

I dedicate this book to my mother, Takako Hamanaka and my husband, Takehisa Ishida who are always incredibly supportive of me. My mother taught me the joy of homemade food. When she was young, her life was very tough as she had to live through a war. She said that she was poor, but she learnt how to cook through using any ingredients around her. My husband, Takehisa, has always encouraged me quietly, and has never denied me of my ambitions.

Acknowledgements

I want to thank:

My baking teacher, Mrs. Chie Kato, for her Swiss roll sponge recipe, which I have introduced in my book. She is a famous baking instructor in Japan, whose fame rivals that of Martha Stewart! She has a refined sense of taste, especially in the area of cake decoration, and her recipes are simple but tasty.

My Singaporean friends: Susan Utama, Law Siew Khee, Emily Cheng, Lin Limei, Clair Wee and Loke Kah Yin; they are not only my students but also my best friends. In Singapore, we spent a lot of time together , sharing recipes, cooking, and dining at many restaurants. I learnt a lot about Singaporean culture from the home parties, gatherings and festive occasions such as Chinese New Year, that they invited me to. I really enjoyed being with them ,and will always feel fortunate to have them as my good friends.

Shermay Lee, who has given me many opportunities to introduce my cooking and baking to Singaporeans. She is a very capable and charming lady who always encourages and supports me.

My Japanese friends who live in Singapore: Shizuka Nagamine, Sachiko Nakamura, Mika Ito, Masako Kusama, Junko Suzuki and Yumiko Suzuki for their friendship, kindness and assistance, especially Shizuka, who supported and assisted me with baking throughout the entire photo shoot for my book. I enjoyed the process because Shizuka always stood by me.

Whoever who has bought my book: I am very happy to have this opportunity to share my passion for baking with you, and I hope you will find delight in sharing my recipes with your family and friends.

Last but not least, God and my guardian angels for giving me a wonderful gift and this opportunity to share my talents. I hope that everyone who reads this book will be able to give their love to others through their baking. May God bless everyone who lives in this beautiful world.

Love,

Keiko

introduction

*When I was young, my mother often baked
simple sweets for my two older brothers and I.*

As we loved sweets, my mother would make them as often as she could in her spare time. I remember her sweets clearly: they may not have been the prettiest, but they were simple and tasty. I was very happy with them. My mother's specialty was pineapple cheesecake. She would bake it for us almost everyday. She also loved making pancakes, doughnuts, custard paste sandwiches, steamed cakes, butter cupcakes—also known as Japanese-style madeleines—and many more. In this book, I will introduce my take on Pineapple Cheesecake and Japanese-style Madeleines, inspired by my mother.

One of my fondest memories is of making doughnuts together with my mother and one of my older brothers. We would knead the dough and make shapes such as baseball bats, balls, rings, braids and more, and then my mother would deep-fry them. We had such a good time together! I started baking on my own when I was nine years old. I was fascinated with making cookies from my mother's small baking book, which was written by an American woman. My brothers would gobble up the cookies I baked, then ask me to bake some more! It was then I discovered how my baking had the ability to make people happy. In return, I was also filled with joy baking for my loved ones and others.

I began studying the art of baking in several baking schools when I turned 21. At 27, I enrolled in The Ritz Escoffier School in Paris. Since then, I have made it a point to visit France, and to continue to learn French pastry recipes every year. I have been teaching baking classes for almost 15 years. However, I don't see myself as a pastry chef, but as a bearer of love and joy through my gift of baking. More than the mere production of pastries, baking can be likened to the act of bringing love and joy to people. It makes me happy that my students, friends and family love my recipes. My students especially love eating and making their own cakes. They bake for their families, friends and also for themselves! Some of my students have gone on to become professionals in the art of baking; one is a pastry chef, another a baking instructor, another the owner of a café, and yet another the owner of a catering business! I am very proud of them, and in turn, I receive constant encouragement and love from them.

There is always plenty of love that goes into the making and baking of a homemade cake. I do love eating cakes and pastries from popular confectionaries, and I appreciate beautiful, complicated cakes and pastries, with many layers, flavours and ingredients, that are like fine works of art. But nothing beats the pleasure of baking simple sweets in the comfort of your own home!

I hope my recipes will bring lots of love and pleasure to everyone who buys this book. More than anything else, it is my sincere desire that you will make your family and friends happy with your baking, just as I have!

Love,

Keiko

baking basics

THINGS TO DO BEFORE YOU START BAKING

1 Read the recipe and understand it

Read the recipe through and make sure you understand it before you start baking. Take note of the ingredients and equipment you will need, and be aware of the time required for putting the recipe together, so you can plan your time.

2 Prepare the ingredients and equipment needed

Make sure you have all the necessary ingredients and equipment on hand before attempting a recipe. As far as possible, always use the freshest and highest quality of ingredients you can find. Weigh the ingredients in advance. I recommend using a digital scale which enables you to measure out ingredients accurately. Some recipes require advance preparation such as bringing ingredients to the right temperature, greasing and lining cake pans, sifting flour, separating eggs yolks from whites, melting chocolate or butter and toasting nuts, which should be done to make the baking process smoother. Once done, you will find that you are halfway through to completing the recipe!

3 Have a neat, clean work space

To work more efficiently, you need a neat and clean space. If your kitchen is small and tends to become overheated like mine, expand your working area with an extra table in the dining room outside the kitchen.

4 Check and adjust the room temperature, if necessary

Room temperature and level of humidity affects the outcome of your baking. If necessary, turn on your air conditioner to lower the temperature and level of humidity.

5 Preheat the oven and create space in the refrigerator and freezer

Make preheating the oven before you start baking a habit. It is fine to let some cakes and cookies sit while the oven warms up, but it is always best to put them into the oven the moment the batter has been mixed. If a cake needs to be cooled down or chilled, make space in the refrigerator or freezer beforehand.

baking equipment

1 Chiffon cake pan or tube pan

This cake pan is made up of two aluminium pieces—an outer ring and a base piece that forms the bottom and the centre tube. It is not advisable to use a non-stick tube pan when baking chiffon cake.

2 Fluted tart tin with removable base

In my recipes, I often use tart tins that are either 20 cm or 22 cm in diameter. A tart or pie this size will typically serve 8–10 persons.

3 Muffin pan and paper muffin cases

My oven is quite small, so I use a 6-hole muffin pan instead of a 12-hole pan. That is why my muffin recipes only make 6 muffins, but you can always double the recipe to make more. I always use paper cases when baking muffins as this makes it easier to remove the muffins from the pan and to serve them.

4 Pound cake moulds

When baking pound cakes, you can use any type of pound cake moulds from those made of tin, aluminium or stainless steel. Take note however, that tin moulds absorb heat easily and will not be ideal if making chilled desserts such as mousse cakes and cheesecakes.

5 Round cake pan with removable base

Cake pans with a removable base allows delicate cakes to be removed easily. Select pans made of aluminium or stainless steel as they can be used for baking or chilling and do not rust easily.

6 Square cake ring without base

Cake rings are useful for making mousse cakes and cheesecakes. Use stainless steel cake rings as they are harder and hold their shape better than aluminium cake rings. Tin moulds tend to absorb heat easily and are not suitable for making chilled desserts.

7 Stainless steel or aluminium tray

Have these on hand to keep ingredients organised, to spread custard cream out for chilling or for placing under a cake rack when dusting with icing sugar or cocoa powder.

8 Swiss roll cake pan or sheet pan

A Swiss roll cake pan is a shallow square pan typically made of aluminium or stainless steel. For my recipes, I use a 28 x 28-cm pan.

9. Flower nail

A flower nail is essential for piping flowers, leaves and other cake decorations. The key to making perfect buttercream or sugar flowers is to coordinate the turning of the nail with the formulation of each flower petal.

10. Metal cutters (plain and fluted)

I prefer using metal cutters to plastic ones, as I find that metal cutters give a cleaner cut which is important for pies and scones, as it makes them rise better. I recommend getting a boxed set that includes cutters in a range of sizes.

11. Measuring spoons

To measure small quantities of ingredients precisely, you must use measuring spoons. It is ideal to have a set made up of ¼ tsp, ½ tsp, 1 tsp and 1 Tbsp sizes. Note that 1 tsp = 5 ml and 1 Tbsp = 15 ml. Stainless steel measuring spoons are more durable than plastic ones which tend to retain food smells. When measuring dry ingredients such as salt and baking powder, be sure to level them off. When measuring liquids such as vanilla extract and liqueur, pour the liquids up to the edge of the spoon.

12. Mixing bowls

Stainless steel bowls are useful for recipes that require setting a bowl over hot or ice water since they have good thermal conductivity. They are easily washed and kept clean, and are very durable. I find the 23 cm bowls and 27 cm bowls very handy.

13. Oval cake pan, fluted tartlet tin and round tartlet tin

Small cake pans and tartlet tins are useful for making miniature treats. These pans are available in a variety of shapes at kitchenware shops.

14. Piping tips

14a Petal decorating tips: These are used for making flower petals. Choose the tips according to the size you want for your flowers.

14b Round, plain 10-cm and 15-cm tips: These are used for piping lines and balls of buttercream for cake decorations.

14c Star-shaped and St. Honore tips: Star-shaped tips can be used to make fancy decorations like stars, shell shapes and zig-zag lines. The St. Honore nozzle is a unique tip used to decorate St. Honore cakes, but can be used to pipe attractive designs on any cake.

15. Non-stick baking mat

Baking mats are heat-resistant, non-stick and reusable. Thick baking mats are best for making macarons as it helps even out the heat distribution. A thin mat can be used in the same way as parchment paper. I use it to line the tart tin when blind baking before adding aluminium weights. This helps ensure that the tart crust is kept even and flat.

16 Aluminium weights

Aluminium weights are reusable and can be easily washed and cleaned after use. When blind-baking tart shells, line the tart tin with aluminium foil or a non-stick baking mat, pressing well into the bottom corners, then add the baking weights. Other types of baking weights include ceramic weights, dried beans or rice.

17 Citrus juicer

A citrus juicer makes juicing citrus fruit very easy. Cut the fruit in half, then squeeze it on the sharp edge of the juicer to extract the juice.

18 Digital kitchen timer (not pictured)

If your oven is not equipped with a timer, invest in a good digital timer to help you churn out perfectly baked cakes.

19 Digital scale

Since precise measurements are very important in baking, I recommend using a digital scale. I prefer using a scale that has a minimum scale unit of less than 1 g and which can weigh up to 2 kg for home baking.

20 Measuring cup

Use clear measuring cups, preferably made of microwave-safe glass, so you can read the measurements at eye level and heat the liquid if necessary. I find it useful to have 2 measuring cups on hand, one in 250 ml and the other in 500 ml measurements.

21 Parchment paper and natural drawing paper

Parchment paper is used to line baking trays and cake pans. It is heat-resistant, non-stick and disposable. Natural drawing paper is the cheaper alternative to parchment paper, but it is not non-stick. I use these sheets to line my work surface so cleaning up is easier. I also sift flour onto parchment or natural drawing paper, so I can lift it up easily and pour it back into the mixing bowl.

22 Piping bags

Piping bags are essential for decorating cakes, and they are also useful for piping cake batter into small cake pans and mousse into glasses. Both disposable plastic piping bags and reusable cloth piping bags are available.

23 Ruler

A ruler is useful when you have to cut cakes into equal layers and measure mould sizes. I prefer using a plastic ruler that can be easily washed and kept clean. A 40-cm ruler is adequate.

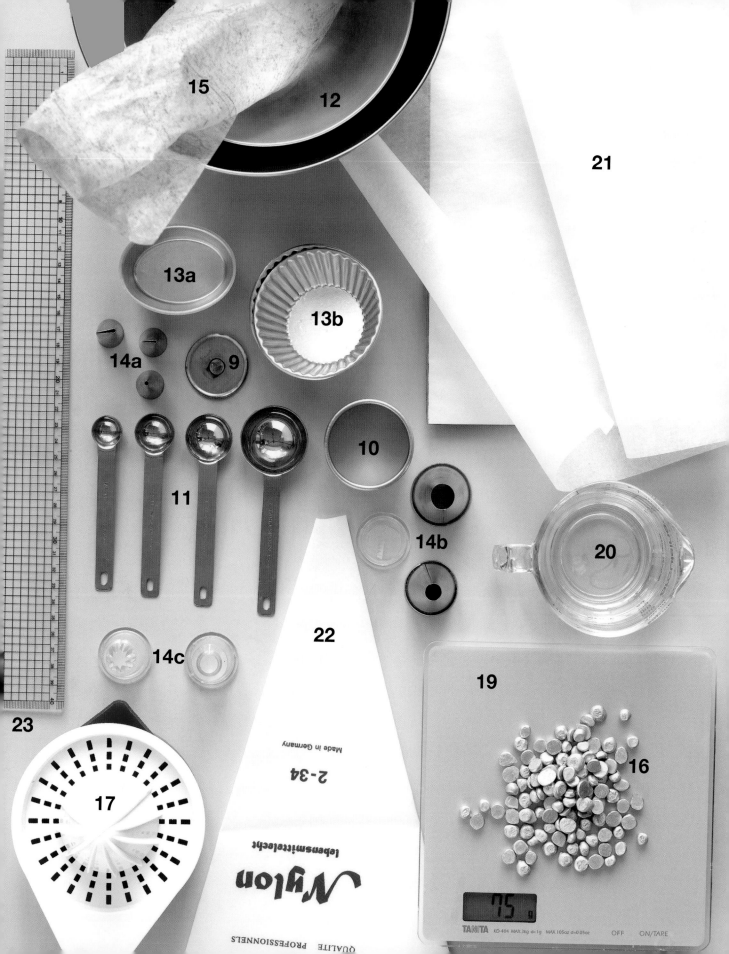

24 Grater

A grater can be used to zest citrus fruit like lemons, limes and oranges. Make sure that you do not grate the fruit too deeply, as the white part of the citrus fruit is very bitter. Graters can also be used to grate hard ingredients such as hard cheese, chocolate and nutmegs.

25 Offset spatula and straight spatula

An offset spatula (25a) is a palette knife with an angled blade. A straight spatula (25b) is a palette knife with a long, flexible metal blade. These spatulas are used to spread and smoothen batter evenly inside cake pans and spread cream on cakes in an even layer. Useful sizes to have are the 26 cm and 18 cm straight spatulas, and 20 cm and 11 cm offset spatulas.

26 Pastry brushes

A small brush (26a, about 2.5-cm width) is useful for buttering small cake pans and ramekins. A medium brush (26b, about 3-cm width) with natural soft bristles is handy for applying egg wash to cookies, pies and bread dough, and for brushing syrup on sponges and glazing jam on cakes. A big brush (26c, about 4-cm width) with natural bristles that are attached to the handle tightly is useful for brushing excess flour from pieces of rolled-out dough.

27 Perforated wooden spatula

When cooking liquids such as custard sauce and jam, I prefer using a perforated wooden spatula with a straight edge. The hole in the spatula makes it easier to stir the sauce or jam.

28 Rolling pin

Choose a wooden rolling pin that is slightly heavy. Its weight will help to flatten and push out dough while rolling it. A pin without a handle offers you the most control. My preference is for a rolling pin which is 45-cm long and 3.5 cm in diameter.

29 Scraper

The humble scraper is often referred to as a friend of the chef. This is a small but indispensable tool. I use it for cleaning floured tabletops, smoothing cookie dough, spreading sponge batter evenly in the cake pan and scooping up cream. Choose a hard plastic scraper.

30 Serrated cake slicer

A long slicer (30a) is very useful in slicing sponge cakes into layers and slicing bread without compressing it. A short slicer (30b) is handy for cutting fruit, nuts, tarts and cakes.

31 Silicone spatula

A silicone spatula is heatproof, which means you can use it to stir cake mixes as well as stir-fry ingredients. It is solid and long-lasting. I prefer using an integrated silicone spatula, which can be easily washed and kept clean, rather than a spatula with a wooden or plastic handle.

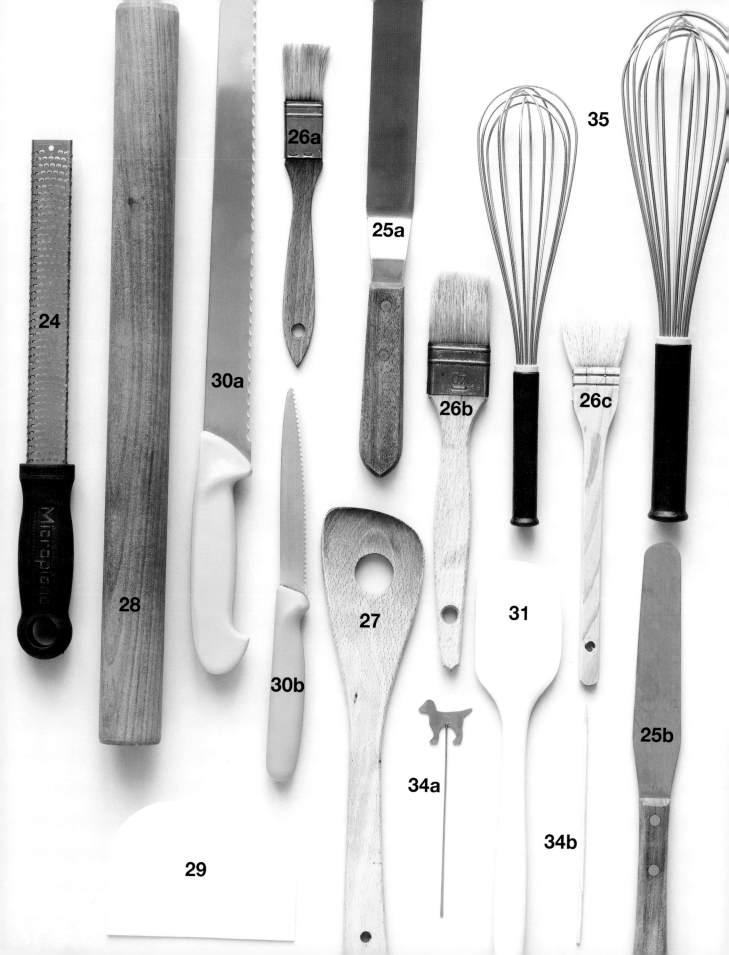

32 Decorating turntable

This is very useful when you need to spread the top and sides of cakes evenly with cream, and when applying decorations. A simple and small plastic turntable is good enough.

33 Saucepans

Use thick-based saucepans when cooking custard creams and sauces, syrups and jams. Saucepans that are at least 9-cm deep are ideal for stirring and mixing ingredients.

34 Cake tester and bamboo skewer

Test if a cake has been adequately baked by inserting a cake tester (34a) or bamboo skewer (34b) into the centre of the cake. The cake tester or bamboo skewer should come out clean.

35 Whisks

Choose stainless-steel whisks with fine and solid wires. My preference is for 27-cm and 35-cm long whisks.

36 Wire strainers

Wire strainers can be used for straining liquids or sifting flours. I use a 16-cm diameter wire strainer (36a) for straining liquid mixtures and sifting flour, and a small wire strainer (36b) for dusting icing sugar or cocoa powder on cakes, pastries and other desserts.

37 Wire racks

Raised wire racks allow air to circulate around freshly baked cakes to cool them down. I find rectangular (28 × 43-cm) and round (30-cm diameter) wire racks most useful.

38 Blowtorch

A blowtorch is useful for unmoulding chilled cakes from cake moulds. It can also be used to caramelise Italian meringues and sugar on the surface of crème brûlées.

39 Electric cake mixer and electric handheld mixer

I can't imagine baking without an electric mixer. There are two types of electric mixers: stand mixers (39a) and portable electric handheld mixers (39b). The handheld mixer is affordable and can be used when beating mixes over a double boiler. However, a handheld mixer has a lower power level than a stand mixer, so it will take longer to whisk or beat a mixture to the required consistency. Having both mixers handy would be ideal.

basic ingredients

EGGS

Egg white powder

Egg white powder is useful to have on hand. I find that adding a little egg white powder when beating egg whites will help strengthen the meringue. To do this, mix the egg white powder with the sugar before adding it to the egg whites. If you add egg white powder to the egg whites without the sugar, it will clump together and will not dissolve. Egg white powder is also very useful when making macarons.

Eggs

In my recipes, I use whole eggs that weigh about 60 g. The weight of the egg white should be about 35 g and the yolk 15–20 g. It is best to choose the freshest eggs possible when baking. The eggs must also be at room temperature, so make sure to remove the eggs from the refrigerator about 30 minutes before you start baking. When separating egg yolks from egg whites, it is easier to use your hands instead of using the cracked shells, as the sharp edges of the shell may pierce the egg yolk. Egg whites can be frozen and kept in the freezer for up to one month.

FLAVOURINGS & INGREDIENTS

Assorted dried fruit

These natural and tasty ingredients are very useful for baking. My favourite dried fruit include Californian dried apricots, Turkish dried figs, as well as dried cranberries, raisins and pitted dried prunes.

Candied fruit

Candied fruit such as citrus peel and cherries add a special touch to baked goods. When purchasing citrus peel, try to choose those that are soft and not bitter. Candied cherries come in festive red and green colours and are perfect for using in Christmas cakes and cookies.

Chestnuts

Fresh chestnuts, chestnut paste and steamed chestnuts are used in the recipes in this book. Fresh chestnuts are seasonal, so substitute with steamed chestnuts (sold in jars) when necessary. Canned French chestnut paste is available all year round and is a good alternative to cream when decorating cakes.

Chocolate

There are so many varieties of chocolate available that you might find it rather difficult to choose a suitable chocolate for baking. My preference is for dark chocolate, white chocolate and French cocoa powder. Dark chocolate is produced by adding cocoa butter and sugar to cocoa without the addition of milk. European standards specify that dark chocolate must contain a minimum of 35% cocoa solids. White chocolate is made with sugar, milk powder and cocoa butter without the cocoa solids. Cocoa power is the non-fat part of cocoa bean, which is ground into a powder. It is unsweetened and very useful for baking. Store chocolate in a cool, dark and dry place. White chocolate tends to spoil easier than dark chocolate, so it is best not to keep white chocolate for too long.

Fruit purée

I often use fruit purée for cakes as they are packed with flavour. Some frozen purées contain added sugar, so read the label and choose one that best suits your taste. Fruit purées come in various pack sizes. I usually get the 1-kg pack as it is more economical and divide it into 100-g portions, placing them in cling wrap, then into freezer bags. Portioning out the purée in advance is very useful, as I only need to thaw the amount I need.

Green tea powder

Green tea powder is made from green tea leaves, which are dried and ground into a fine powder. Traditionally used for brewing tea, green tea powder is now commonly used for flavouring pastries. Store in the freezer to prolong its shelf life.

Japanese pumpkin

Japanese pumpkin (*kabocha*) is smaller than the Western variety of pumpkin. It has dark green skin and orange flesh that is sweet with a firm texture, making it ideal for baking.

Japanese red beans

Japanese red beans (*azuki*) are rich in protein and fibre. Red beans are regarded as a very nutritious food in Japanese cuisine. Although used in both savoury and sweet dishes, red beans are predominantly used in making Japanese-influenced Western pastries.

Japanese sweet potato

The Japanese sweet potato (*satsuma imo*) has reddish-purple skin and pale yellow flesh. Its sweetness makes it ideal for using in cakes and pastries.

Liqueur

The addition of liqueur gives cakes a rich flavour, and I especially like using cherry, orange and coffee liqueurs, and brandy and rum. When using liqueur, I use drinking liqueur rather than those made for confectionery purposes.

Mincemeat

Mincemeat is essentially a mixture of dried and candied fruit, sugar, spices and rum used to make pies and tarts. Ready-made mincemeat is sold in specialty supermarkets.

Vanilla flavouring

The vanilla bean is the second most expensive spice after saffron. With its complex floral aroma, it is an extremely popular and versatile spice. Madagascar produces high-grade vanilla beans which are often referred to as "Bourbon vanilla". Use this if available, although vanilla extract and vanilla paste are more affordable. Vanilla beans can be frozen for better storage.

GRAINS & FLOUR PRODUCTS

Carob

Carob comes from the pea plant and is grown in eastern Mediterranean regions. Carob powder is sometimes used as an alternative for chocolate and cocoa power although its flavour is significantly different. Despite the difference in flavour, carob is high in calcium, fibre and iron, and low in calories, making it a healthy alternative.

Cornmeal

Coarse wholegrain corn flour is usually called cornmeal. I use cornmeal when making savoury muffins and doggy treats.

Oatmeal

Oatmeal is a product of ground whole oat groats. It is high in fibre, vitamins and minerals, and can help lower cholesterol. It adds texture and flavour to baked goods.

Flours

There are many varieties of white flour available and the names they go by may be different in different countries. White flour is made from the endosperm of heat grains and there are two types of wheat: soft wheat and hard wheat. Soft wheat contains less protein than hard wheat, so white flour produced from the former contains less protein than the latter. White flour is classified by the amount of protein it contains. When the proteins in flour mixes with water, gluten is produced. This gluten gives the dough its elastic structure and taste, so different types of flour will produce baked goods with differing textures.

Cake flour is a low-gluten flour. It is made from soft wheat and contains 6–8 per cent protein. It is good for making sponge cakes, chiffon cakes and Swiss rolls.

Pastry flour is also known as top four and is similar to cake flour. These types of flour contain 8–10 per cent protein and are suitable for making soft and light-textured cakes such as sponge and chiffon cakes, and lighter cookies and butter cakes. In France, flour that contains less than 9 per cent protein is called Type 45.

Plain flour is also known as all-purpose flour. It contains 9–11 per cent protein and is suitable for making puff pastry, cookies, butter cakes and pancakes and for using in cooking. In France, flour that contains 9–11 per cent protein is called Type 55.

Bread flour is a high-gluten flour. It contains 12–14 per cent protein which gives the baked product its shape and structure. High gluten flours are good for making bread.

Wholemeal flour is made from the entire wheat grain. It is high in fibre, vitamins and minerals. It is suitable for making healthy, low-calorie breads, cakes and pastries.

NUTS & SEEDS

Almonds

The almond is a versatile nut that can be used in many ways. Spanish and Californian almonds are popularly used in baking. They come in many different forms, including whole, sliced, slivered, diced and ground. Almonds are best kept in the freezer to ensure freshness.

Black and white sesame seeds

Sesame seeds have a strong nutty flavour and aroma which is brought out when toasted. Sesame seeds can be used whole or ground in baking. As they have a high oil content, keep refrigerated to extend their shelf-life.

Walnuts

Shelled walnuts are used in many recipes. Californian and Chinese walnuts are readily available. My preference is for Californian walnuts as Chinese ones tend to have a bitter taste. Toasting them lightly before use brings out their flavour. Walnuts must be kept dry and preferably refrigerated. I always keep them in the freezer as they oxidise easily.

OILS

Canola oil and safflower oil

Canola oil and safflower oil are good alternatives to olive oil for baking. They are relatively flavourless, unlike olive oil, which has a distinct flavour. Thus, they are suitable for baking light cakes like chiffon cakes. They also contain oleic acid, which is good for lowering cholesterol levels.

Olive oil

There are two kinds of olive oil—extra virgin and regular. Extra virgin olive oil has a stronger fragrance than regular olive oil. It contains oleic acid and vitamin E, which is a powerful antioxidant to forestall aging. Olive oil is a good substitute for saturated fats, and can be used as a healthy substitute. It matches well with chocolate.

Unsalted butter

It is best to use unsalted butter when baking so as to control the amount of salt in the cake. The butter must be at room temperature for baking and not melted. Ideally, butter should be kept in the refrigerator in an airtight container because it tends to absorb odours quite easily. Butter can also be kept in the freezer for a longer period of time.

SOY & DAIRY PRODUCTS

Cream cheese

Cream cheese is commonly used to make cheesecake. I prefer using French cream cheese to American cream cheese as it is less salty and has a softer texture.

Whipping cream

There are several types of whipping cream, and they sometimes go by different names. Choose the right whipping cream according to the fat content labelled on the packet. Depending on the recipes of the recipe, I use French whipping cream, which contains around 35 per cent fat and Australian thickened cream, which contains around 45 per cent fat.

Milk

I use fresh whole milk when baking as it has a richer, fresher taste than low-fat and UHT milk. Substitute as necessary according to your dietary requirements and preferences.

Mascarpone cheese

Mascarpone cheese is a very popular Italian cream cheese. It has about 80 per cent fat and is not overly sour or salty. Mascarpone is an essential ingredient in making tiramisu.

Bean curd, soy bean powder and soy milk

Soy bean curd is processed from soy beans, and contains a lot of textured vegetable protein. It is low in fat, which makes it good for health. There are two types to choose from: soft bean curd and firm bean curd. It is advisable to drain bean curd before using in baking as it has a high water content which will affect the outcome of the cake.

Soy bean powder (*kinako*) has a fragrant, nutty flavour and is popularly used in many Japanese sweets.

Soy milk is produced by soaking dry soy beans and grinding them with water, and has about the same amount of protein as cow's milk. It is rich in vitamins B and E and has no cholesterol. Soy milk is a good substitute for cow's milk, and is a vegetarian option.

STARCHES & LEAVENERS

Agar-agar

Agar-agar (*kanten*) is a natural gelling agent that is derived from a fern-like seaweed that grows in the Pacific and Indian oceans. It can set in room temperature, without having to be refrigerated. Sold freeze-dried, agar-agar comes in two forms: long filaments and powder. Agar-agar has no flavour, aroma or calories. It is an excellent setting agent and suitable for making healthy cakes and desserts.

Baking powder

Baking powder is a dry chemical leavening agent often used in baking. The most commonly used baking powder today is double-acting baking powder. Double-acting baking powder contains two acid salts: one which reacts at room temperature and the other which reacts at high temperature. If too much baking powder is added, it might leave a bitter aftertaste. Aluminium-free baking powder will not leave this aftertaste.

Corn flour and potato flour

These flours can be used as a thickener in many recipes. I often use it together with flour to give my cakes a lighter texture. Corn flour is also known as cornstarch.

Gelatin

Gelatin comes in two forms: powder and sheet. I prefer using gelatin sheets as it is more manageable. Gelatin is extracted from the collagen found inside an animal's skin and bones, and is made of protein. It melts when heated and solidifies when cool. Some fruit such as pineapple and kiwi contain an enzyme which breaks down protein, thus causing gelatin to lose its gelling abilities. I prefer using gelatin that contains 2–3 per cent moisture. Check the label on the packaging.

SWEETENERS

Agave syrup

Agave syrup is produced in Mexico. It is a light brown syrup with a texture thinner than honey, but is sweeter than honey and sugar. It can be used as a substitute for sugar in baking and is a popular alternative sweetener for people who have dietary restrictions or diabetes.

Beet sugar

Beet sugar is made from the sugar beet which is grown in temperate areas. It is another popular alternative sweetener for people who have dietary restrictions.

Brown rice syrup

Brown rice syrup has a mild, buttery flavour and a delicate sweetness which makes it a healthy alternative to regular sugar. It is a very popular sweetener for people who are on macrobiotic diets.

Castor (superfine) sugar

Castor sugar is a vital ingredient in baking. Made from cane sugar, the crystals are finer than regular white sugar and thus dissolves faster when mixed.

Glucose

Glucose is a thick, clear syrup that is used in a variety of recipes to help cakes retain their moisture. It also controls the formation of sugar crystals. Light corn syrup and golden syrup are good substitutes for glucose.

Honey

Honey is another alternative sweetener to sugar. It helps cakes retain moisture while giving them a bouncy texture. The flavours and colours of honey varies according to the source of the nectar from which it is made. Acacia, clover, orange and lavender honey are suitable for use in baking.

Icing (confectioner's) sugar

Icing sugar is regular granulated sugar that is ground to a very fine powder. It contains 1–2 per cent corn flour which helps to prevent it from clumping together due to humidity. The presence of corn flour in icing sugar renders it unsuitable for use in cold desserts such as jellies, as it affects appearance and taste. If using pure icing sugar, sift it before use.

Light brown sugar and dark brown sugar

When you want to add more flavour and give some colour to your cakes, use brown and dark brown sugar. Although it is also made from cane sugar, brown sugar has more minerals than castor sugar, and it contains purified molasses.

Maple syrup

Maple syrup is made from the sap of sugar maple trees and is mainly produced in Canada. It is golden brown in colour and has a delicate flavour. Maple syrup is the preferred topping for pancakes, waffles and French toast. It can also be used in a variety of baked goods.

basic recipes

swiss roll sponge

Makes one 28 x 28-cm cake

Eggs 3

Castor (superfine) sugar 60 g

Pastry flour or top flour 50 g, sifted twice

1. Preheat oven to 200°C. Line a 28 x 28-cm flat square cake pan with parchment paper.

2. Using a clean bowl, beat eggs with a whisk. Add sugar, then place bowl over a pot of simmering water and mix well.

3. When egg mixture is warm, use an electric mixer and beat on high speed until light and fluffy. Reduce speed to low and continue beating for about 1 minute. Gently fold in flour with a spatula.

4. Pour batter into prepared cake pan and spread evenly with a scraper. Place cake pan on a tray and bake for 10–13 minutes.

5. When Swiss roll sponge is done, remove from pan and place in a big plastic bag to cool.

This simple Swiss Roll Sponge recipe can be used for the Banana Caramel Swiss Roll (page 106), Green Tea Tiramisu (page 84), Bean Curd Cheesecake (page 90), French-style Strawberry Cake (page 110), Chestnut Cake (page 114), Decoration Birthday Cake (page 116) and Pineapple Yoghurt Cheesecake (page 138).

TIPS

Tip 1: Use high heat (about 200°C) when baking a sheet of thin sponge, and low heat when baking a thick sponge (about 160° to 170°C). You should switch and rotate the tins halfway through the baking time to ensure even baking. If your oven is not fan-assisted, you might need to make shallow slits on the surface of the batter for a thick sponge, or it might brown too quickly while leaving the sponge under baked. The small slits enable the inner moisture to evaporate and to bake the centre of the sponge.

Tip 2: By adding heat to the egg mixture, more air can be incorporated easily when the mixture is whipped.

Tip 3: By reducing the speed of the mixer, the volume of the egg mixture is stabilised and less volume is lost when the flour is folded in.

Tip 4: When folding in flour, keep turning the bowl and scoop up the mixture from the centre and bottom of the bowl. Fold until the mixture becomes glossy but take care not to over-mix the batter.

Tip 5: Baking the sponge on an additional tray prevents the bottom of the sponge from browning too quickly.

Tip 6: Cooling the sponge in the plastic bag helps it to retain its moisture.

soufflé roll sponge
Makes one 28 x 28-cm cake

Egg 1

Egg yolks 3

Vanilla extract 1 tsp

Unsalted butter 35 g

Pastry flour or top flour 60 g, sifted twice

Fresh whole milk 60 g

Egg whites 3

Castor (superfine) sugar 85 g

1. Preheat oven to 180°C. Line a 28 x 28-cm flat square cake pan with parchment paper.

2. Combine egg, egg yolks and vanilla extract in a small bowl and beat lightly. Set aside.

3. Place butter in a small saucepan, and heat gently until melted. Add flour to melted butter and cook through. Transfer butter-flour mixture to a bowl, then add egg mixture a little at a time. With a spatula, mix into a smooth batter. Add milk and mix to incorporate. Strain batter and set aside.

4. To make meringue, place egg whites in a clean bowl and beat until foamy. Add half the sugar and continue beating for a few minutes, then add remaining sugar and beat until egg whites are glossy and stiff peaks form.

5. Add one-third of meringue to batter and fold in lightly, then add remaining meringue and fold through until just incorporated. Pour batter into prepared cake pan and spread evenly with a scraper. Place cake pan on a tray and bake for 20 minutes.

6. When cake is done, remove from pan and place in a big plastic bag to cool.

This is another variation of the Swiss Roll Sponge. It is a bit more complicated to make but produces a light cake with a lovely springy and fluffy texture. You can use this recipe for Green Tea Soufflé Swiss Roll (page 74), Banana Caramel Swiss Roll (page 106), Green Tea Tiramisu (page 84), Bean Curd Cheesecake (page 90), French-style Strawberry Cake (page 110), Chestnut Cake (page 114), Decoration Birthday Cake (page 116) and Pineapple Yoghurt Cheesecake (page 138).

TIPS

Tip 1: The Soufflé Roll Sponge is slightly thicker and contains more moisture than the simple Swiss Roll Sponge (page 34), hence it needs to be baked at medium heat.

Tip 2: The gluten content of the flour makes the sponge hard. Cooking flour with butter weakens the gluten content in the flour, resulting in a cake with a light, springy and fluffy texture.

Tip 3: The meringue is essential for the cake to rise, so it must be stiff and stable.

genoise sponge

Makes one 18-cm round cake

Pastry flour or top flour 115 g

Eggs 170 g

Castor (superfine) sugar 130 g

Glucose 15 g

Unsalted butter 30 g, softened

Fresh whole milk 45 g

Vanilla extract 1 tsp

1. Preheat oven to 170°C. Line a 18-cm round cake pan with a removable base with parchment paper. Sift flour twice.

2. Using a clean bowl, beat eggs with a whisk. Add sugar and glucose, then place bowl over a pot of simmering water and mix well.

3. When egg mixture is warm, beat on high speed until light and fluffy. Reduce speed to low and continue beating for about one minute. Gently fold in flour with a spatula.

4. Combine butter, milk and vanilla in a bowl and place over a pot of simmering water. Once butter has melted, stir through to mix.

5. Add one-sixth of egg batter to butter mixture and mix well. Add butter mixture to egg batter and fold through evenly.

6. Pour batter into prepared baking pan and bake for about 40 minutes.

7. Once cake is done, remove from the pan and place on a wire rack in a plastic bag to cool.

This is a thick, moist sponge cake with a very fine texture. You can use this recipe for Japanese-style Strawberry Cake (page 108).

TIPS

Tip 1: Use high heat (about 200°C) when baking a thin sponge and low heat when baking a thick sponge (about 160° to 170°C). Switch and rotate the tins halfway through the baking time to ensure even baking. If your oven is not fan-assisted, when baking a thick sponge, you might need to make shallow slits on the top crust, as it might brown too quickly while leaving the sponge under baked. The slits will enable the moisture inside the cake to evaporate and allow the centre of the sponge to be baked.

Tip 2: When mixing sugar and eggs or egg yolks, always mix them immediately after adding them together, otherwise the yolks will cover the sugar grains and the sugar will not dissolve. The addition of glucose helps keep the cake moist. By adding heat to the egg mixture, more air can be incorporated easily when the mixture is whipped.

Tip 3: By reducing the speed of the mixer, a stable egg mixture with fine foam is obtained, and less volume is lost when the flour is folded in. To test if you have achieved the right consistency, scoop up the mixture and use the spatula or a whisk to "draw" a line on it. The batter should pool in a ribbon-like pattern (page 38, middle picture).

Tip 4: When folding in the flour, keep turning the bowl and scoop up the mixture from the centre and bottom of the bowl. Fold until the mixture becomes glossy. Take care not to over-mix the batter.

Tip 5: Cooling the sponge in a plastic bag helps it to retain its moisture.

biscuit sponge

Makes about 20 fingers

  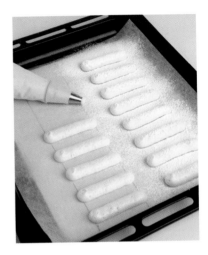

Eggs 2

Castor (superfine) sugar 60 g

Pastry flour or top flour 60 g

Vanilla bean ½, split lengthwise and scraped for seeds, or use 1 tsp vanilla extract or paste

1. Line a baking tray with parchment paper. Preheat oven to 200°C.

2. Sift flour twice. Separate egg whites and yolks. Beat yolks lightly and add half portion of the sugar and all the vanilla. Whisk until mixture thickens and becomes pale yellow in colour.

3. To make meringue, place egg whites in a clean bowl and beat until foamy. Add in remaining sugar and beat until stiff peaks are formed and egg whites are glossy.

4. Add one-third of meringue into egg yolk mixture and fold in lightly. Add sifted flour and fold well, then add remaining meringue and fold through just until incorporated.

5. Spoon batter into a piping bag fitted with a 1-cm piping tip. Pipe 7-cm long fingers onto baking tray, keeping them slightly apart. Dust generously with icing sugar, then bake for 7–10 minutes.

Biscuit sponge is basically an egg sponge that is piped into 'fingers', which is why baked sponge fingers are also known as ladyfingers. As the texture of the biscuit sponge is coarser than that of Genoise Sponge (page 38), it absorbs moisture well and is often used in desserts assembled with cream mousse and jelly. You can use this recipe and technique for French-style Strawberry Cake (page 108), Pineapple Yoghurt Cheesecake (page 138) and Green Tea Tiramisu (page 84).

TIPS

Tip 1: When baking small cakes such as biscuit sponge, use high heat. If baked at low heat, a longer baking time is needed and the sponge gets dry easily.

I use an oven with upper and lower heating elements for even baking of biscuit sponge. Another way to ensure even baking is to rotate the tins halfway through the baking.

Tip 2: In order to pipe the biscuit sponge neatly, the sponge mixture must be firm and stable, not runny. The egg yolk and egg white mixture must be beaten well.

Tip 3: Adding only one-third of the meringue in the beginning is essential because the specific gravities of the meringue and the egg yolk mixture are different, making them hard to mix together.

Adding this initial one-third helps to bridge the difference. The flour must be folded to make gluten, which adds springiness to the sponge.

Tip 4: Biscuit sponge fingers are dusted with icing sugar to make them crispy and to prevent them from turning dark brown. After dusting, the batter must be baked immediately because the sugar will melt and cause the sponge to burn easily if left aside for too long.

special biscuit sponge

Makes one 28-cm square cake

Pastry flour or top flour 40 g

Corn flour (cornstarch) 20 g

Unsalted butter 35 g, softened

Egg whites 90 g

Castor (superfine) sugar 80 g

Egg yolks 80 g

1. Preheat oven to 200°C. Line a 28 x 28-cm flat square cake pan with parchment paper.

2. Sift flours twice. Melt butter over a pot of simmering water or in a microwave oven.

3. To make meringue, place egg whites in a clean bowl and beat until foamy. Add one-quarter of the sugar and beat for a while, then add remaining sugar and beat until stiff peaks form and egg whites are glossy. Add egg yolks and mix well.

4. Sift both flours into the bowl and fold using a spatula. Pour melted butter into the batter and fold well.

5. Pour batter into the prepared pan and spread evenly with a scraper. Place pan onto a baking tray and bake for 10–13 minutes.

6. When cake is done, remove from pan and place in a big plastic bag to cool.

You can use this recipe and technique for Bean Curd Cheesecake (page 90), French-style Strawberry Cake (page 110) and Pineapple Yoghurt Cheesecake (page 138).

TIPS

Tip 1: Use high heat (about 200°C) when baking a thin sponge and low heat when baking a thick sponge (about 160° to 170°C). Switch and rotate the tins halfway through the baking time to ensure even baking. If your oven is not fan-assisted, when baking a thick sponge, you might need to make shallow slits on the top crust, as it might brown too quickly while leaving the sponge under baked. The slits will enable the moisture inside the cake to evaporate and allow the centre of the sponge to be baked.

Tip 2: When making a meringue, do not add sugar to the egg whites at the start. It will take a long time to whip because the egg whites will become very heavy. Whip the egg whites first to create some volume, then add the sugar. If the quantity of sugar is large, add a little at a time. When adding egg yolks, do not over-mix as the fat content from the egg yolks will destroy the meringue bubbles.

Tip 3: When folding in the flour, rotate the bowl continuously and scoop up the mixture from the bottom of the centre of the bowl. Fold until the mixture becomes glossy.

Tip 4: Placing the cake pan on an additional tray in the oven will prevent the bottom of the sponge from browning too quickly.

Tip 5: Cooling the sponge in a plastic bag will help it to retain its moisture.

vanilla chiffon cake

Makes one 20-cm cake

Pastry flour or top flour 80 g

Egg yolks 5

Castor (superfine) sugar 20 g

Water 60 g

Canola oil 60 g

Vanilla bean 1, split lengthwise and scraped for seeds, or use 1 tsp vanilla extract or paste

MERINGUE

Castor (superfine) sugar 20 g

Corn flour (cornstarch) 10 g

Egg whites 5, about 180 g

1. Preheat oven to 160°C. Sift flour twice.

2. Place egg yolks and sugar in a bowl and beat well. Add water, canola oil, and vanilla and stir to incorporate. Add flour and mix well, until the batter becomes sticky.

3. To make meringue, combine sugar and corn flour. Beat egg whites until foamy. Add half the sugar-corn flour mixture and continue beating for a few minutes, then add remaining sugar-corn flour mixture and beat until egg whites are glossy and stiff peaks form.

4. Add one-third of meringue into egg yolk mixture and fold in lightly, then add remaining meringue and fold to incorporate completely.

5. Pour batter into an ungreased 20-cm chiffon cake pan and bake cake for 40–50 minutes.

6. When cake is done, remove from oven and turn it over, leaving it to cool.

7. Once cake has cooled completely, carefully run a knife or spatula around the sides of the cake to loosen it before inverting onto a wire rack.

For other chiffon cake recipes, refer to Green Tea Chiffon Cake (page 78), Black Sesame Chiffon Cake (page 80) and Soy Bean Chiffon Cake (page 82).

TIPS

Tip 1: When baking a thick sponge like chiffon cake, use low heat (about 160°-170°C). You should switch and rotate the pans halfway through the baking time to ensure the cakes bake evenly. If your oven is not fan-assisted, when baking a thick sponge you might need to make shallow slits on the top crust, as it might brown too quickly while leaving the sponge under baked. The slits will enable the moisture inside the cake to evaporate and allow the centre of the sponge to be baked.

Tip 2: The oil, water, egg yolk and flour must be well blended in order to build up the gluten structure, so that the cake is 'springy'.

Tip 3: When making a meringue, do not add sugar to the egg whites at the start. It will take a long time to whip because the egg whites will become very heavy. Whip the egg whites first to create some volume, then add the sugar. If the quantity of sugar is large, add a little at a time. When adding egg yolks, do not over-mix as the fat content from the egg yolks will destroy the meringue bubbles.

Tip 4: Adding only one-third of the meringue in the beginning is essential because the specific gravities of the meringue and the egg yolk mixture are different, making them hard to mix

together. Adding this initial one-third helps to bridge this difference.

Tip 5: Use an ungreased cake pan for chiffon cake. A greased cake pan will hinder the cake from rising to its full volume.

Tip 6: The baked chiffon cake must be turned over, as it is very light in texture, and leaving it right side up will cause the top of the cake to sink.

Tip 7: To unmould chiffon cake, insert the spatula along the sides of the cake, then turn the cake pan around the spatula to loosen the cake. This will prevent the spatula from damaging the delicate cake.

choux puffs

Makes about 15 puffs

Pastry flour or top flour 75 g

Water 75 g

Fresh whole milk 50 g

Unsalted butter 50 g, cut into small cubes

Sugar a pinch

Salt a pinch

Egg 2–3, at room temperature, lightly beaten

1. Preheat oven to 200°C. Line a baking tray with parchment paper. Sift flour once.

2. In a small saucepan, combine water, milk, butter, sugar and salt. Bring to a boil over medium-high heat, then immediately remove from heat.

3. Using a wooden spoon, quickly stir in flour until combined and mixture comes together in a ball. Return to heat and cook, stirring constantly until the mixture leaves the sides of the saucepan and a film forms on the bottom of the pan.

4. Transfer mixture to a clean bowl. Add eggs one at a time, beating with a wooden spoon until egg is fully incorporated before adding the next. (Alternatively, use an electric mixer fitted with a paddle attachment.)

5. Test if the batter is ready by scooping it up using a wooden spoon. The batter should hang down and form a smooth triangular shape (see picture 3 above). If it does not, the batter needs a little more egg.

6. Pour batter into a piping bag fitted with a 1-cm plain piping tip. Pipe out 5-cm circles onto lined baking tray and gently smoothen out the pointed peaks with a moistened finger.

7. Bake for about 20 minutes at 200°C, then reduce heat to 180°C and continue baking for another 20 minutes.

Choux means "cabbage" in French. This puffs are so named because they resemble cabbage heads. Choux pastry dough needs a high amount of moisture and stickiness to create the hollow centre in the puffs. The dough's stickiness is due to the starch found in flour, and the high heat it is exposed to when baked. You can use this recipe for Japanese-style Cream Puffs (page 64).

TIPS

Tip 1: Choux pastry requires baking at high heat for it to rise. This is why they are baked at a high temperature for the first 20–25 minutes until they reach maximum height. The oven temperature is then reduced and the puffs are baked for another 20 minutes to dry them completely.

Tip 2: To ensure that the choux pastry rises, the dough must be strong, stretchy and glue-like. To achieve this, there must be sufficient moisture and heat, so ensure that the milk and water mixture is boiling hot before adding the flour.

Tip 3: Add the eggs one at a time while the dough is still warm, or the dough will become too soft and the puffs will not rise adequately.

Tip 4: The dough should look glossy and not be too runny.

shortcrust pastry crust

Makes one 20-cm or 22-cm pie crust

Cold unsalted butter 60 g,
 cut into small cubes

Pastry flour or top flour 100 g

Castor (superfine) sugar 1/4 tsp

Salt 1/8 tsp

Ice-cold water 50 g

1. Combine butter cubes and flour in a plastic bag. Place in the freezer overnight.

2. Using a food processor, pulse butter and flour mixture, sugar and salt until the mixture resembles coarse breadcrumbs. Add water and mix until a smooth dough is formed.

3. Place dough on a floured surface and knead lightly. Leave dough to rest in the refrigerator overnight.

4. Roll out dough to a thickness of 5 mm on a floured surface. Brush away excess flour, then place dough over a 20-cm or 22-cm fluted tart tin with a removable base. Gently press dough into the tin. Roll a rolling pin over the top of the tin to trim any excess dough. Prick dough with a fork, then leave to rest for about 5 minutes in the freezer before baking.

5. Preheat oven to 200°C.

6. Place a sheet of aluminium foil over the chilled dough (without covering the edges of the dough), pressing it well into the bottom edges. Place baking weights into the tart tin and bake for 20 minutes. Carefully remove weights and aluminium foil when pastry just begins to change colour around the edges, then continue baking until light golden brown for another 10 minutes.

7. If tart shell is to be filled and baked again, cover with aluminium foil and fill with pie weights, and bake only for 10 minutes, then bake according to instructions in recipe.

8. Remove from heat and leave to cool on a wire rack.

This recipe for shortcrust pastry uses the rubbing-in method, where butter and flour are rubbed together to form a breadcrumb-like mixture. It is essential that you use cold butter in this recipe, as softened butter will result in pastry that is not crisp. You can use this recipe for the Fruit Tart (page 122) and Apple and Mincemeat Pies (page 126).

TIPS

Tip 1: Ensure that all the ingredients are chilled as the butter should not be melted. For those attempting to make shortcrust pastry for the first time, I recommend using a food processor to blend the ingredients because it is hard to control and obtain the appropriate temperature otherwise. The dough must be rested in the fridge since the gluten it contains makes it shrink easily if used immediately after it has been made.

Tip 2: If the dough is too soft, refrigerate to chill before rolling it out. Dust the work surface well with flour to prevent the dough from sticking.

sweet shortcrust pastry crust

Makes one 20-cm or 22-cm pie crust

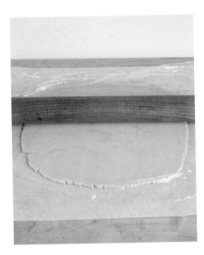

Unsalted butter 70 g, at room temperature and softened

Icing (confectioner's) sugar 35 g

Salt a pinch

Vanilla extract 1 tsp

Eggs 20 g

Ground almonds 20 g

Pastry flour or top flour 130 g, sifted

1. Beat butter, icing sugar, salt and vanilla extract with an electric mixer until just combined.

2. Add egg and beat well. Add ground almonds and mix well. Add flour and fold through completely. Using a bench scraper, mix batter until a smooth dough is formed. Wrap dough in cling film, then place in the refrigerator to rest for at least 3 hours.

3. Unwrap dough and place on a non-stick baking mat. Cover dough with cling film and roll out to a thickness of 3–5 mm. Place dough (with cling film still intact) into a 20-cm or 22-cm fluted tart tin with removable base and gently press it into the tin without stretching it. Remove and discard cling film.

4. Roll the rolling pin over the top of the tin to trim excess dough. Prick dough with a fork, then rest for about 5 minutes in the freezer before baking.

5. Preheat oven to 180°C.

6. Place a sheet of aluminium foil over the chilled dough (without covering the edges of the dough), pressing it well into the bottom edges. Place baking weights into the tart tin and bake for 20 minutes. Carefully remove weights and aluminium foil when pastry just begins to change colour around the edges, then continue baking until light golden brown for another 10 minutes.

This is a popular sweet cookie dough which can be used for making tarts or sugar cookies. If making sugar cookies, use cookie cutters of desired shapes to cut out cookies. You can use this recipe for: Sweet Potato Tart (page 98), Pumpkin Tart (page 100), Pine Nut Tart (page 120) and Caramel Nut Tartlets (page 124).

TIPS

Tip 1: The butter must be at room temperature, but not half-melted. If the butter is melted, the resulting cookies will be very hard.

Tip 2: Do not over-whip the butter with the eggs. Doing so will incorporate more air, which will cause the pastry to be too crumbly.

Tip 3: The dough must be rolled while covered with cling film and placed on a non-stick baking mat because it gets soft quickly. If soft dough is rolled out on a floured surface, it will absorb excess flour easily and become hard. When dough gets too soft, let it chill in the refrigerator before rolling again.

Tip 4: Resting the dough helps relax the gluten and prevents the dough from shrinking during baking.

pound cake

Makes one 19 x 9 x 8-cm cake

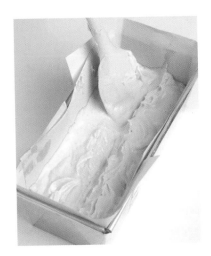

Pastry flour or top flour 150 g

Baking powder 1/8 tsp

Unsalted butter 150 g, softened

Icing (confectioner's) sugar 150 g

Salt 1/8 tsp

Eggs 3, about 150 g, beaten lightly

Lemon 1, grated for zest

1. Preheat oven to 170°C. Line a 19 x 9 x 8-cm loaf tin with parchment paper. Sift flour and baking powder together twice.

2. Beat butter, icing sugar and salt together in an electric mixer until light, fluffy and pale. Takes about 10 minutes. Gradually add eggs and beat well.

3. Add flour and baking powder mixture and fold through completely using a spatula. Surface of batter should be glossy and smooth.

4. Pour batter into prepared loaf tin and make a lengthwise 'cut' in the middle with a spatula. Bake for about 50 minutes.

5. When cake is done, remove it from the loaf tin and place on a wire rack to cool. Wrap with cling film before storing.

This is a simple cake that is ideal for beginners to try their hand at. Its basic composition consists of the same amount of butter, sugar, flour and eggs, known as "*quatre-quarts*" in French. I added lemon zest for flavour, but you can replace it with vanilla if you wish.

TIPS

Tip 1: Pound cakes require a medium temperature and a fairly long baking time.

Tip 2: The butter should be at room temperature but not half-melted. If it is too soft, the batter will not be fluffy because it will not combine with air. I prefer icing sugar over castor sugar as it combines with butter faster.

Tip 3: The eggs must be at room temperature and not cold. This will ensure that they are incorporated into the batter easily.

Tip 4: By making a 'cut' in the middle of the batter, the pound cake will develop a straight crack after baking. If the top of your cake browns too fast while you are baking, you might need to make a lengthwise shallow slit, or cover it with some aluminium foil to prevent it from burning any further.

pastry cream

Fresh whole milk 200 g

Vanilla bean 1/2, split lengthwise and scraped for seeds

Egg yolks 3

Castor (superfine) sugar 50 g

Pastry flour or top flour 20 g, sifted

1. Add milk, vanilla bean and seeds to a saucepan and bring to a boil.

2. In a clean bowl, beat egg yolks and sugar together until mixture is pale yellow in colour. Add flour and mix well.

3. Add hot milk to the egg mixture and fold through. Remove vanilla bean from mixture.

4. Return egg and milk mixture to the saucepan and bring to a boil over high heat, stirring constantly. Continue mixing until mixture becomes smooth and glossy, then remove the saucepan from heat.

5. Transfer pastry cream to a tray, cover with cling film and place in the freezer to cool but do not freeze. Before use, gently beat cream with an electric mixer until smooth and creamy.

6. Pastry cream can be kept in the refrigerator for up to 2 days.

This is a very popular pastry cream used in many pastries and desserts. It is essential that you use the freshest eggs and milk to make this cream. You can use this recipe for Green Tea Cream Puff and Black Sesame Cream Puff (page 64), French-style Strawberry Cake (page 110) and Fruit Tart (page 122).

TIPS

Tip 1: Infuse the vanilla bean in the hot milk to get the most out of its flavour.

Tip 2: The egg mixture must be well mixed before adding the hot milk. Otherwise, the eggs will cook too quickly.

Tip 3: Because pastry cream contains flour, it must be cooked over high heat to ensure that it is cooked through completely.

Tip 4: Pastry cream must be cooled rapidly to prevent the growth of bacteria, which is why it is placed in the freezer. It should be kept refrigerated at all times.

custard sauce

Fresh whole milk 200 g

Vanilla bean ½, split lengthwise and scraped for seeds

Castor (superfine) sugar 50 g

Egg yolks 3

1. In a saucepan, heat milk over low heat with vanilla bean and seeds and half the sugar. The milk does not need to be boiled as is the case with pastry cream, as there is no flour in the recipe.

2. In a clean bowl, beat egg yolks and remaining sugar until a light emulsion is formed.

3. Add a little of the warm milk into egg mixture and mix well.

4. Add egg and milk mixture to remaining milk in the saucepan and cook over gentle heat, stirring continuously until it thickens. Remove vanilla bean from mixture.

You can use this recipe for Green Tea Ice Cream and Black Sesame Ice Cream (page 68) and Keiko-style Mango Pudding (page 140).

TIPS

The custard will start to thicken at around 60°C, and it must be cooked to 80°C. To test if you have achieved the right consistency, coat the back of a wooden spoon with the custard and run your finger down the middle. You should be able to see a distinct line. If not, your custard is not thick enough. However, don't over-cook the custard as it will curdle and become lumpy. If this happens, use an electric handheld blender to blend away the lumps.

buttercream

Unsalted butter 400 g, at room temperature

Egg whites 140 g

Icing (confectioner's) sugar 140 g

Orange or cherry liqueur 1 Tbsp

1. Beat butter until pale and creamy. Butter must be at room temperature but not melted. If butter is melted, the buttercream will become too soft and will not be able to keep its shape.

2. Using a clean bowl, beat egg whites until foamy. Add half the sugar and continue beating. When egg whites have achieved some volume, add remaining sugar and continue to beat until egg whites are glossy and stiff peaks form.

3. Add meringue to butter and mix thoroughly. Add orange or cherry liqueur and fold in well.

This is a simple buttercream that is ideal for home bakers and beginners. You can use this recipe in Green Tea Dacquoise (page 70) and Coffee Dacquoise (page 72), Green Tea Soufflé Swiss Roll (page 74), Chiffon Cake (page 44), Austrian Coffee Cream Sponge Cake (page 112) and Birthday Cake (page 116).

TIPS

Make sure that the whipped butter and meringue are mixed together very well to avoid the buttercream separating.

whipped cream

Whipping cream (35% fat) 200 g

Castor (superfine) sugar 15 g

Vanilla extract ¹/₂ tsp

1. Combine ingredients in a clean bowl. Place bowl over a larger bowl filled with ice cubes and water.

2. Using an electric mixer, whip cream at medium speed until stiff peaks form but cream is still smooth. Do not over-whip or the cream will become grainy and separate to form butter.

TIPS

Tip 1: It is essential to whip the cream over a bowl of iced water to keep it cold, otherwise the cream will become warm and curdle easily.

Tip 2: Use fresh (single) whipping cream for this recipe, not the long-life variety of whipping cream. The whipping cream must also have at least 35% fat.

new creations
(western pastries with a japanese touch)

japanese-style cream puffs

Makes about 15 puffs

Choux puffs (page 46) 1 quantity

Whipping cream (35% fat) 150 g

Castor (superfine) sugar 2 tsp

Green tea leaves or
black sesame seeds 2 Tbsp

PASTRY CREAM

Fresh whole milk 400 g

Egg yolks 6

Castor (superfine) sugar 100 g

Pastry flour or top flour 20 g, sifted

Corn flour (cornstarch) 20 g, sifted

PASTRY CREAM FLAVOURING

Green tea powder 8 g, or store-bought
black sesame paste 60 g

1. Prepare choux puffs (page 46). Before baking puffs, sprinkle them with green tea leaves or black sesame seeds.

2. Prepare pastry cream (page 54). When pastry cream is cooled, beat with an electric mixer until smooth and creamy. Add green tea powder or black sesame paste and mix well. Transfer to a piping bag fitted with a 1-cm round piping tip.

3. To assemble cream puffs, slice one-quarter off the top of choux puffs. Pipe in green tea or black sesame pastry cream.

4. Place a mixing bowl into a larger bowl half-filled with iced water. Place whipping cream and castor sugar in the mixing bowl and whip until stiff peaks form.

5. Transfer whipped cream into a piping bag fitted with star-shaped piping tip, then pipe it over the green tea or black sesame filling.

6. Replace the tops of puffs and serve or store in an airtight container in the refrigerator.

financiers, two flavours

Makes about 16 cakes

ALMOND FINANCIER

Pastry flour or top flour 50 g

Corn flour (cornstarch) 5 g

Baking powder 1/2 tsp

Egg whites 130 g

Castor (superfine) sugar 130 g

Ground almonds 50 g

Vanilla extract 1/2 tsp

Salt a pinch

Unsalted butter 130 g

GREEN TEA VARIATION

Green tea powder 10 g

1. Preheat oven to 220°C. Lightly grease 16 small cake moulds, each about 5.5 x 7.5-cm, with a little softened butter and place them on a baking tray. Sift flour, corn flour and baking powder together twice. If making green tea financiers, add green tea powder and sift twice.

2. Place egg whites into a clean bowl and beat lightly. Add sugar and mix well, followed by ground almonds, vanilla extract (only if making almond financiers), flour mixture and salt, mixing well after each addition. Be careful not to over-mix. Set aside.

3. Brown butter in a small saucepan over medium-low heat, whisking frequently until fragrant and golden brown in colour. Pour into a mixing bowl and place into a larger bowl half-filled with iced water to stop butter from cooking further and burning.

4. Add browned butter to egg white mixture and mix well. Transfer batter into a piping bag fitted with a 1-cm plain piping tip. Pipe batter into prepared cake moulds.

5. Bake financiers for 10–15 minutes until they are light golden in colour. Remove the cakes from the moulds and cool on a wire rack before serving. Financiers will keep in an airtight container at room temperature for up to 5 days, or for up to 1 month in the freezer.

ice cream, two flavours

Serves 8

GREEN TEA ICE CREAM

Fresh whole milk 200 g

Egg yolks 3

Castor (superfine) sugar 80 g

Green tea powder 10 g

Whipping cream (35% fat) 100 g

BLACK SESAME ICE CREAM

Fresh whole milk 200 g

Egg yolks 3

Castor (superfine) sugar 60 g

Black sesame paste 50 g

Whipping cream (35% fat) 100 g

1. Heat milk in a saucepan almost to the boiling point, then remove from heat and set aside.

2. In a mixing bowl, beat egg yolks and sugar until pale yellow in colour. If making green tea ice cream, add green tea powder and mix well.

3. Add warm milk and mix well. Return mixture to the same saucepan and heat very gently, stirring constantly, until it thickens to form a custard.

4. Transfer custard into a mixing bowl. Place bowl in a larger bowl half-filled with iced water to cool. If making black sesame ice cream, add black sesame paste and mix well. Set aside.

5. In a chilled bowl, whip whipping cream until stiff peaks form. Add whipped cream to custard and fold through. Transfer mixture to an ice cream maker and churn according to the manufacturer's instructions.

6. Store in the freezer or serve immediately.

green tea dacquoise

Makes about 16 cakes

BISCUIT DACQUOISE

Ground almonds 180 g

Icing (confectioner's) sugar 80 g + more for dusting

Green tea powder 10 g

Castor (superfine) sugar 40 g

Egg white powder 2 g

Egg whites 200 g

GREEN TEA CREAM

Unsalted butter 100 g, at room temperature

Egg whites 35 g

Icing (confectioner's) sugar 35 g

Green tea powder 5 g

1. Preheat oven to 180°C. Line a baking tray with parchment paper. Sift ground almonds, icing sugar and green tea powder together with a coarse sieve twice. Set aside.

2. Combine castor sugar and egg white powder. Beat egg whites until foamy. Add sugar and egg white powder mixture and beat until egg whites are glossy, with stiff peaks.

3. Add sifted ground almond mixture to the meringue and fold in gently to make the dacquoise batter.

4. Transfer batter into a piping bag fitted with a 1.5-cm round piping tip. Pipe out small discs (about 3.5-cm in diameter) onto parchment paper. Dust with icing sugar twice and bake for 15–20 minutes until dacquoise rises and surface becomes dry.

5. Make green tea cream. Beat butter until pale and creamy. Using a clean bowl, beat egg whites until foamy. Add half the sugar and continue beating. When egg whites have achieved some volume, add remaining sugar and continue to beat until egg whites are glossy and stiff peaks form. Add meringue to butter and mix thoroughly. Add green tea powder and fold in well. Transfer green tea buttercream into a piping bag fitted with piping tip.

6. Pipe cream onto flat side of the dacquoise discs. Sandwich with another disc, flat-side down.

7. For best results, make dacquoises and assemble them the day before serving and leave to chill in the refrigerator. They can be kept for up to 3 days.

Dacquoises are dainty little French cakes that have a light crumb but give a full, rounded mouthful without any heaviness. In this unusual pairing, the slight bitterness of green tea perfectly complements, and offsets the sweet, toasty nuttiness of the dacquoise.

coffee cream dacquoise

Makes about 16 cakes

Rum-soaked raisins*

BISCUIT DACQUOISE

Ground almonds 180 g

Icing (confectioner's) sugar 80 g +
    more for dusting

Castor (superfine) sugar 40 g

Egg white powder 2 g

Egg whites 200 g

COFFEE CREAM

Unsalted butter 100 g

Egg whites 35 g

Icing (confectioner's) sugar 35 g

Instant coffee granules 2 tsp

Rum 2 tsp

1. Preheat oven to 180°C. Line a baking tray with parchment paper. Sift ground almonds and icing sugar together with a coarse sieve twice.

2. Combine castor sugar and egg white powder. Beat egg whites until foamy. Add sugar and egg white powder mixture and beat until egg whites are glossy, with stiff peaks.

3. Add sifted ground almond mixture to the meringue and fold in gently to make the dacquoise batter.

4. Transfer batter into a piping bag fitted with a 1.5-cm piping tip. Pipe out small discs (about 3.5-cm in diameter) onto parchment paper. Dust with icing sugar twice and bake for 15–20 minutes.

5. Make coffee cream. Beat butter until pale and creamy. Using a clean bowl, beat egg whites until foamy. Add half the sugar and continue beating. When egg whites have achieved some volume, add remaining sugar and continue to beat until egg whites are glossy and stiff peaks form. Add meringue to butter and mix thoroughly. Dissolve coffee granules in rum, then add to buttercream mixture and fold through Transfer coffee cream into a piping bag fitted with 1-cm piping tip.

6. Pipe cream onto the flat side of the dacquoise discs. Sprinkle about 3 rum-soaked raisins over cream, then sandwich with another disc, flat-side down.

7. For best results, make the dacquoises and assemble them the day before serving and leave to chill in the refrigerator. They can be kept for up to 3 days.

*RUM-SOAKED RAISINS

1. Poach any amount of raisins in a pot of hot water and strain. Stir-fry the raisins without oil to dry them out or pat dry with kitchen paper.

2. Transfer raisins to a jar and pour in just enough rum to cover them. Soak the raisins overnight before use. They can be kept at room temperature for up to 1 year.

The velvety undertones of coffee sings through the rum-laced cream, making these dainty little cakes a decadent treat indeed!

green tea soufflé swiss roll

Makes one 28-cm Swiss roll

Soufflé roll sponge (page 36) 1 quantity

Green tea powder 5 g, sifted

Red bean paste* 120 g

Whipping cream (35% fat) 100 g

Castor (superfine) sugar 2 tsp

*RED BEAN PASTE

Red beans (*azuki*) 500 g

Japanese sugar (*jo haku tou*) 430 g

Salt 1/2 tsp

1. Prepare soufflé roll sponge (page 36), adding green tea powder to flour.

2. Prepare red bean paste. Wash red beans well, then bring to boil in a pot of water. Drain and place red beans in a saucepan.

3. Pour in enough water to cover red beans and bring to a simmer over low heat for about 2 hours, skimming off the foam. When the beans are soft, remove from heat and drain.

4. Return red beans to saucepan and add sugar. Cook over low heat and stir constantly for 5–10 minutes. Add salt and mix well. Spread paste out on a tray to cool. Weigh out 120 g and store remaining paste in an airtight container for up to 2 weeks in the refrigerator, or up to 2 months in the freezer.

5. Whip whipping cream and castor sugar in a chilled mixing bowl until stiff peaks form (page 60).

6. Assemble Swiss roll. Turn cooled soufflé sponge onto a clean work surface. Peel off parchment paper from the bottom of the sponge. Spread whipped cream in an even layer over the entire sponge. Spoon red bean paste in a line across Swiss roll, nearer to one edge of cake.

7. Gently roll up sponge from the edge near red bean paste to make a Swiss roll. Wrap with cling film and place in the freezer to chill and set before serving.

green tea sablé cookies

Makes about 50 cookies

Pastry flour or top flour 240 g, chilled

Green tea powder 15 g

Unsalted butter 150 g, at room
  temperature

Icing (confectioner's) sugar 130 g

Salt a pinch

Egg yolks 2

Granulated sugar as needed

Egg white 1, beaten

Green tea leaves (optional) as needed

1. Sift flour and green tea powder together twice. Set aside.

2. Beat butter, icing sugar and salt until soft and creamy. Add egg yolks and mix well. Add flour and green tea powder mixture and fold in with a spatula. Cover dough with cling film and chill in the refrigerator for about 15 minutes.

3. Divide chilled dough in half. Place a portion of dough on a large sheet of parchment paper, then shape it into a log about 3.5 cm in diameter. Wrap log with parchment paper. Repeat with other portion of dough. Refrigerate dough until firm. If not using immediately, wrap with cling film and freeze. Cookie dough can be kept for up to 2 months in the freezer.

4. Preheat oven to 150°C. Cut logs into 7-mm thick rounds. Dip edges in granulated sugar.

5. Place cookies on a baking tray lined with parchment paper. Brush a little egg white over the cookies and scatter a few green tea leaves on top if desired.

6. Bake for about 25 minutes, then remove and leave to cool on a wire rack before serving. Store cookies in an airtight container at room temperature for up to 10 days.

green tea chiffon cake

Makes one 20-cm cake

Pastry flour or top flour 70 g

Green tea powder 10 g

Egg yolks 5

Castor (superfine) sugar 20 g

Water 70 g

Canola oil 60 g

MERINGUE

Castor (superfine) sugar 90 g

Rice flour or corn flour (cornstarch)
 10 g

Egg whites 180 g, about 5 eggs

GREEN TEA CREAM

Whipped cream (page 60) 1 quantity

Green tea powder 7 g

1. Preheat oven to 160°C.

2. Sift flour and green tea powder together twice. Combine egg yolks and sugar in a bowl and mix well. Add water and canola oil and blend together. Add flour and green tea powder mixture and mix until batter becomes sticky. Set aside.

3. Make meringue. Combine sugar and rice or corn flour. Beat egg whites until foamy. Add half the sugar and flour mixture and continue beating for a few minutes, then add remaining sugar and flour mixture and beat until egg whites are glossy, with stiff peaks.

4. Add one-third of meringue to egg yolk mixture and fold in lightly, then add remaining meringue and fold to incorporate completely.

5. Pour batter into an ungreased 20-cm chiffon cake pan. Place in the oven and bake for 40–50 minutes. When cake is done, remove from oven and turn the pan over. Leave cake to cool in pan.

6. Once cake has cooled completely, carefully run a knife or spatula around the sides of the cake to loosen it before inverting onto a wire rack (page 44).

7. Make green tea cream. Prepare whipped cream (page 60), then mix whipped cream with green tea powder.

8. Cover chiffon cake with green tea cream using a spatula and a decorating turntable. Decorate as desired. Slice to serve.

black sesame chiffon cake

Makes one 20-cm cake

Pastry flour or top flour 70 g

Egg yolks 5

Brown sugar 20 g

Black sesame paste 20 g

Water 60 g

Canola oil 40 g

Whipped cream (page 60) 1 quantity

Black sesame seeds (optional) 20 g

MERINGUE

Castor (superfine) sugar 90 g

Rice flour or corn flour (cornstarch) 10 g

Egg whites 180 g, about 5 eggs

GARNISH (OPTIONAL)

Black sesame seeds

1. Preheat oven to 160°C. Sift flour once.

2. Combine egg yolks, brown sugar and black sesame paste in a bowl and mix well. Add water and canola oil and blend together. Add flour and mix until batter becomes sticky, then fold in black sesame seeds.

3. Make meringue. Combine sugar and rice or corn flour. Beat egg whites until foamy. Add half the sugar and flour mixture and continue beating for a few minutes, then add remaining sugar and flour mixture and beat until egg whites are glossy, with stiff peaks.

4. Add one-third of meringue into egg yolk mixture and fold in lightly, then add remaining meringue and fold to incorporate completely. Do not over-mix as the sesame paste in the mixture will cause the volume of the chiffon cake to decrease, thus making it heavy.

5. Pour batter into an ungreased 20-cm chiffon cake tube pan. Bake for 40–50 minutes. When cake is done, remove from oven and turn the pan over. Leave cake to cool in pan.

6. Once cake has cooled completely, carefully run a knife or spatula around the sides of the cake to loosen it before inverting onto a wire rack (page 44).

7. Prepare whipped cream (page 60).

8. Cover chiffon cake with whipped cream using a spatula and a decorating turntable. Sprinkle black sesame seeds over if desired. Slice before serving.

soy bean chiffon cake

Makes one 20-cm cake

Pastry flour or top flour 50 g

Egg yolks 5

Brown sugar 20 g

Water 60 g

Canola oil 60 g

Soy bean powder (*kinako*) 50 g

MERINGUE

Castor (superfine) sugar 90 g

Rice flour or corn flour (cornstarch) 10 g

Egg whites 180 g, about 5 eggs

RED BEAN CREAM

Whipped cream (page 60) 1 quantity

Red bean paste (page 74) 125 g

1. Preheat oven to 160°C. Sift flour once.

2. Combine egg yolks and brown sugar in a bowl and mix well. Add water and canola oil and blend together. Add flour and mix until batter becomes sticky, then fold in soy bean powder.

3. Make meringue. Combine sugar and rice or corn flour. Beat egg whites until foamy. Add half the sugar and flour mixture and continue beating for a few minutes, then add remaining sugar and flour mixture and beat until egg whites are glossy, with stiff peaks.

4. Add one-third of meringue into egg yolk mixture and fold in lightly, then add remaining meringue and fold to incorporate completely.

5. Pour batter into an ungreased 20-cm chiffon cake tube pan. Place in the oven and bake for 40–50 minutes. When cake is done, remove from oven and turn it over, leaving it to cool.

6. Once cake has cooled completely, carefully run a knife or spatula around the sides of the cake to loosen it before inverting onto a wire rack (page 44).

7. Make red bean cream. Prepare whipped cream (page 60) and red bean paste. Mix whipped cream with red bean paste.

8. Cover chiffon cake with red bean cream using a spatula and a decorating turntable. Decorate as desired. Slice to serve.

green tea tiramisu

Serves 10

Biscuit sponge (page 40) 1 quantity

MASCARPONE CHEESE FILLING

Egg yolks 40 g, about 2 eggs

Castor (superfine) sugar 70 g

Mascarpone cheese 250 g

Whipping cream (35% fat) 100 g

Egg whites 70 g

Green tea powder 10 g + extra for dusting

Hot water 90 g

1. Prepare biscuit sponge (page 40).

2. Prepare mascarpone cheese filling. Combine egg yolks and 30 g sugar in a bowl and beat until mixture thickens and becomes pale yellow in colour. Add mascarpone cheese and mix well.

3. Whip whipping cream in a chilled bowl until stiff peaks form. Add whipped cream to the mascarpone cheese mixture and fold through.

4. Make meringue. Place egg whites in a clean bowl and beat until foamy. Add remaining sugar and beat until stiff peaks form and egg whites are glossy. Fold into mascarpone cheese mixture.

5. Place green tea powder in a small bowl and mix with hot water a little at a time. Stir until completely dissolved. Quickly dip both ends of each biscuit sponge in the green tea mixture, then place in a medium serving dish such as a 27-cm oval dish, or into individual serving glasses.

6. Spread half of mascarpone cheese filling in a layer over soaked biscuit sponges. Dip more biscuit sponges into green tea mixture and place on top of mascarpone cheese layer. Spoon over remaining mascarpone cheese filling.

7. Dust generously with green tea powder and refrigerate until required. Tiramisu can be kept refrigerated for up to 2 days.

Forget the usual coffee-based version; give this Japanese-inspired tiramisu a try—I guarantee there will be calls for second helpings when you serve this up for dessert!

dark brown sugar swiss roll

Makes one 28-cm Swiss roll

WHITE CHOCOLATE CREAM

Whipping cream (35% fat) 150 g

White chocolate 50 g

SPONGE

Pastry flour or top flour 40 g

Rice flour 15 g

Unsalted butter 40 g

Egg whites 140 g

Castor (superfine) sugar 20 g

Dark brown sugar (*kuro zatou*) 70 g

Egg yolks 90 g, about 5 eggs

1. Prepare white chocolate cream a day in advance. In a saucepan, bring whipping cream to a boil. Place white chocolate in a bowl and pour hot cream over. Wait for 30 seconds, then stir the mixture with a spatula until smooth. Set aside to cool, then chill in the refrigerator overnight.

2. On the day of baking, preheat oven to 200°C. Sift both flours together twice. Line a 28 x 28-cm flat square cake pan with parchment paper and place on a baking tray.

3. Melt butter in a pot of simmering water or in a microwave oven. Set aside.

4. Place egg whites into a clean bowl and beat until foamy. Add castor sugar and one-third brown sugar and continue beating for a few minutes, then add remaining brown sugar and beat until egg whites are glossy and stiff peaks form.

5. Add egg yolks and fold lightly. Add sifted flours and fold gently with a spatula, then add hot melted butter and fold through. Pour batter into prepared cake pan and spread evenly with a scraper. Bake for 10–13 minutes.

6. When cake is done, unmould from pan and place it into a plastic bag to cool. (The cake can be kept in the plastic bag until the next day if you are not using it immediately.)

7. To assemble, whip white chocolate cream until light and fluffy using an electric handheld mixer. Turn cooled sponge onto a clean work surface. Peel off the parchment paper from the bottom of the sponge. Spread the white chocolate cream in an even layer over the sponge.

8. Gently roll up the sponge to make a Swiss roll. Wrap with cling wrap and chill in the freezer to allow the Swiss roll to set. Slice to serve.

So simple but so sublime; the dark brown sugar lends an unusual flavour and richness to this Swiss roll recipe.

polvorones

Makes about 16 cookies

Pastry flour or top flour 110 g

Unsalted butter 100 g

Icing (confectioner's) sugar 40 g +
more for dusting

Ground almonds 50 g

SOY BEAN VARIATION

Soy bean powder (*kinako*) 60 g

1. Preheat oven to 150°C. Sift flour and bake for 25 minutes. Stir occasionally while baking, then remove from oven and leave to cool.

2. Keep oven heated at 150°C.

3. Beat butter and icing sugar together until soft. Add ground almonds and mix well. If making soy bean polvorones, add soy bean powder at this point and mix well. Add flour and mix with a spatula until a smooth dough forms.

4. Roll dough out to a thickness of 1-cm. Cut out shapes using your preferred pastry cookie cutter and place them on a baking tray lined with parchment paper.

5. Bake for 20–25 minutes. Remove from heat and cool on a wire rack.

6. Dust cooled polvorones with icing sugar. Serve or store in an airtight container to keep them crisp.

A polvorone is a traditional Spanish cookie. It is also known as Mexican wedding cookies as it is traditionally served at weddings and celebrations. Made with flour, sugar, milk and nuts, the cookie is soft in texture and melts in the mouth.

Polvorones are traditional Spanish cookies that are served during festive occasions like Christmas. Their melt-in-your-mouth texture makes them extremely popular.

bean curd cheesecake

Makes one 18-cm cheesecake

SOY BEAN SPONGE

Pastry flour or top flour 40 g

Soy bean powder (*kinako*) 20 g + more
   for sprinkling

Unsalted butter 30 g

Egg whites 90 g

Castor (superfine) sugar 60 g

Light brown sugar 20 g

Egg yolks 80 g

Sugar syrup 2 Tbsp (made using 25 g
   sugar and 50 g water)

BEAN CURD CREAM

Cream cheese 230 g

Light brown sugar 10 g

Castor (superfine) sugar 70 g

Silken bean curd 230 g, drained

Double (heavy) cream (45% fat) 50 g

Sour cream 50 g

Soy milk 100 g

Gelatin sheets 6 g, soaked in iced water
   to soften

1. Preheat oven to 200°C. Line a 28 x 28-cm flat square cake pan with parchment paper.

2. Sift flour and soy bean powder together twice. Melt butter over a pot of simmering water or in a microwave oven.

3. Mix castor and brown sugars together. To make meringue, place egg whites in a clean bowl and beat until foamy. Add half the sugar and beat for a while, then add remaining sugar and beat until stiff peaks form and egg whites are glossy. Add egg yolks and mix well.

4. Sift both flours into the bowl and fold in using a spatula. Pour melted butter into the batter and fold well. Pour batter into prepared cake pan and spread batter evenly with a scraper. Place pan onto a tray and bake for 10–13 minutes.

5. When cake is done, remove from pan and place in a big plastic bag to cool. When cake is cool, peel paper and brown skin from sponge.

6. Place an 18 x 18-cm square cake ring on cake and press down to cut out cake. Remove trimmings. Place cake still in cake ring on a baking tray and brush cake with sugar syrup. Set aside.

7. Prepare bean curd cream. Place cream cheese, brown sugar and castor sugar into a food processor and blend until creamy. Add bean curd, double cream, sour cream and soy milk and blend thoroughly.

8. Place softened gelatin sheets in a small bowl and melt over a pot of simmering water. Add to cream cheese mixture and mix well. Pour mixture into cake ring over soy bean sponge and smooth it out evenly with an offset spatula. Leave refrigerated overnight.

9. To unmould cake, warm sides of cake ring with a warm towel or a blowtorch. To slice cake, use a warm knife. Sprinkle with soy bean powder. Serve immediately.

pumpkin cheesecake

Makes one 18-cm cheesecake

Walnuts 30 g

Wheat crackers 70 g

Unsalted butter 40 g, melted + more for
greasing cake pan

Japanese pumpkin 250 g, skinned
and seeded

Brown sugar 90 g

Cream cheese 220 g

Ground cinnamon 1/2 tsp

Vanilla extract or paste 1/2 tsp

Whipping cream (35% fat) 50 g

Eggs 2

Egg yolk 1

1. Without preheating oven, toast walnuts at 150°C for 20 minutes. Chop walnuts into small pieces. Set aside.

2. Increase oven heat to 170°C. Prepare an 18-cm round cake pan with a removable base. Grease lightly with softened butter.

3. Place wheat crackers and toasted walnuts in a food processor and lightly pulse into fine crumbs. Add melted butter and mix well. Transfer crumbs to prepared cake pan and spread evenly. Press down well and place in the refrigerator or freezer to set.

4. Place pumpkin flesh in a microwave-safe plate and cook in the microwave oven for 5 minutes at 600w (Medium). Place cooked pumpkin and brown sugar into a food processor and blend well. Add cream cheese, ground cinnamon, vanilla and whipping cream and blend. Pour out into a mixing bowl. Beat eggs and egg yolk and add to blended pumpkin. Mix lightly. Do not over-mix.

5. Pour pumpkin mixture over set cracker base and bake for 40–50 minutes, until surface is light brown and centre of cheesecake feels springy to the touch.

6. Gently run a knife along the edge of cheesecake and leave to cool on a wire rack. Cover with cling film and chill in the refrigerator overnight.

7. On day of serving, unmould cheesecake and slice into even pieces using a warmed knife.

black sesame cream jelly

Serves 6

Fresh whole milk 300 g

Store-bought black sesame paste 50 g

Castor (superfine) sugar 35 g

Gelatin sheets 5 g, soaked in iced water
to soften

Whipping cream (35% fat) 40 g

Black sugar for sprinkling, chopped

1. Combine milk, sesame paste and sugar in a small saucepan and bring to
a boil.

2. Add softened gelatin sheets and whipping cream. Mix well. Pour mixture into
6 small cups and chill in the refrigerator until set.

3. Serve jelly topped with chopped black sugar.

sesame cookies

Makes about 40 cookies

Pastry flour or top flour 220 g

White sesame seeds 50 g

Black sesame seeds 50 g

Unsalted butter 100 g, softened

Icing (confectioner's) sugar 100 g

Salt $1/8$ tsp

Egg yolks 40 g, about 2 eggs

1. Sift flour, then place in the freezer to chill. Without preheating oven, bake white and black sesame seeds at 150°C for 10–15 minutes. Set aside to cool.

2. Beat butter, icing sugar and salt until soft and creamy. Add egg yolks and mix well. Add flour and sesame seeds and fold in with a spatula.

3. Divide dough in half. Transfer each half to a piece of parchment paper and shape into a 12 x 7 x 2.5-cm rectangle. Wrap dough in cling film and chill in the refrigerator for at least 3 hours.

4. Preheat oven to 160°C.

5. Slice chilled cookie dough into 5–7 mm thick bars. Place on a baking tray lined with parchment paper. Bake for about 20 minutes until golden brown. Let cool on a wire rack.

6. Store cookies in an airtight container to keep them crisp.

sweet potato tart

Makes one 22-cm tart

SWEET SHORTCRUST PASTRY

Unsalted butter 70 g

Brown sugar 35 g

Salt a pinch

Eggs 20 g

Soy bean powder (*kinako*) 20 g

Pastry flour or top flour 70 g, sifted

Rice flour 30 g, sifted

SWEET POTATO FILLING

Sweet potatoes 400 g, peeled and diced

Castor (superfine) sugar 70 g

Brown sugar 40 g

Vanilla extract 1/2 tsp

Egg yolks 3

Unsalted butter 30 g

Whipping cream (35% fat) 160 g

Black sesame seeds 2 Tbsp, toasted at 150°C for 10 minutes

EGG WASH

Egg yolk 1

Water as needed

1. Prepare sweet shortcrust pastry. Beat butter until soft and creamy. Add brown sugar, salt, egg and soy bean powder and mix well. Add both flours and fold in with a spatula. Wrap dough in cling wrap and rest in the refrigerator for 3 hours.

2. Unwrap dough and place on a non-stick baking mat. Cover dough with cling film and roll out to a thickness of 3–5 mm. Remove non-stick baking mat and place dough (with cling film still intact) into a 22-cm fluted tart tin with a removable base. Gently press dough into tin without stretching dough. Remove and discard cling film.

3. Roll the rolling pin over the top of the tin to remove excess dough. Prick dough with a fork, then rest for about 5 minutes in the freezer before baking.

4. Preheat oven to 180°C.

5. Place a sheet of aluminium foil over the chilled dough (without covering the edges of the dough), pressing it well into the bottom edges. Place baking weights into the tart tin and bake for 20 minutes. Carefully remove weights and aluminium foil when pastry just begins to change colour around the edges, then continue baking until light golden brown for another 10 minutes.

6. Prepare sweet potato filling. Place diced sweet potatoes in a microwave-safe dish and cook for about 8 minutes at 600w (Medium) until soft.

7. Place cooked sweet potatoes into a food processor and blend into a purée. Add castor sugar, brown sugar, vanilla, egg yolks and unsalted butter and blend again. Add whipping cream gradually and mix until combined.

8. Mix black sesame seeds into sweet potato mixture and pour filling into prepared tart shell.

9. Make egg wash by mixing egg yolk and a little water in a small bowl. Brush over tart.

10. Bake tart for about 30 minutes until the top turns golden brown. Leave to cool on a wire rack.

11. Dust with icing sugar, if desired, and slice to serve.

The humble sweet potato really comes into its element in this simple tart recipe!

pumpkin tart

Makes one 20-cm tart

Sweet shortcrust pastry crust (page 50) 1 quantity

Whipped cream (page 60) 1 quantity

PUMPKIN FILLING

Japanese pumpkin 200 g, peeled and seeds removed

Castor (superfine) sugar 30 g

Gelatin sheets 4 g, soaked in iced water to soften

Egg yolk 1

Fresh whole milk 25 g

Whipping cream (35% fat) 65 g

Vanilla extract $1/2$ tsp

Ground cinnamon a pinch

MERINGUE

Egg whites 25 g

Castor (superfine) sugar 15 g

1. Prepare sweet shortcrust pastry crust using a 20-cm tart tin with fluted edges and a removable base (page 50). Prepare whipped cream (page 60).

2. Prepare pumpkin filling. Cut pumpkin flesh into cubes. Place in a microwave-safe dish and cook in the microwave oven for about 5 minutes at 600w (Medium).

3. Place cooked pumpkin, sugar and softened gelatin sheets into a food processor and pulse until well-blended. Add egg yolk, milk, whipping cream, vanilla and ground cinnamon and blend well. Set aside.

4. Make meringue. Beat egg whites until foamy. Add half the sugar and continue beating for a few minutes, then add remaining sugar and beat until egg whites are glossy and stiff peaks form.

5. Fold meringue into pumpkin filling, then pour into tart shell. Refrigerate for about 1 hour until set.

6. Spoon whipped cream into a piping bag fitted with a 1-cm round tip. Pipe cream evenly over chilled tart and decorate as desired. Slice to serve.

japanese milky madeleines

Makes 18 small cakes

Pastry flour or top flour 120 g

Rice flour or corn flour (cornstarch) 20 g

Milk powder 15 g

Baking powder ¹/₂ tsp

Honey 15 g

Hot water 1 Tbsp

Unsalted butter 100 g

Double (heavy) cream (45% fat) 50 g

Vanilla extract 1 tsp

Eggs 140 g

Salt a pinch

Japanese sugar (*jo haku tou*) or castor (superfine) sugar 150 g

1. Preheat oven to 170°C. Line a 9-hole muffin tray with paper cases. Sift together flours, milk powder and baking powder. Combine honey and hot water in a small bowl.

2. Place butter, cream and vanilla in a heatproof bowl. Place over a pot of simmering water and heat, stirring until butter is melted. Set aside.

3. In another heatproof bowl, beat eggs and salt with a whisk. Add sugar and place the bowl over a pot of simmering water and mix well. When egg mixture is warm, use an electric mixer to beat on high speed until light and fluffy. Reduce speed to medium and continue beating for about 1 minute. Add honey and mix well.

4. Gently fold in flour mixture with a spatula. Add cream and butter mixture and fold until just incorporated.

5. Spoon batter into a piping bag fitted with a 1-cm piping tip. Pipe batter into prepared baking tray. Bake for about 25 minutes until madeleines are light golden in colour. Cool on a wire rack.

6. Store madeleines in an airtight container at room temperature for up to 5 days, or up to 1 month in the freezer.

These simple butter cakes are a classic
Western-influenced treat in Japan.
They are perfect for afternoon tea,
paired with your favourite hot beverage.

all-time favourites

banana caramel swiss roll

Makes one 28-cm Swiss roll

Swiss roll sponge (page 34) 1 quantity

Ripe bananas 2

CARAMEL CREAM

Castor (superfine) sugar 50 g

Whipping cream (35% fat) 50 g

WHIPPED CREAM

Whipping cream (35% fat) 120 g

Castor (superfine) sugar 1 tsp

1. Prepare Swiss roll sponge (page 34).

2. Make caramel cream. Place sugar in a saucepan and heat until it caramelises. Carefully pour cream into the saucepan while stirring slowly with a spatula. Mix until smooth. Leave to cool.

3. Make whipped cream (page 60). Combine whippig cream and sugar in a clean bowl. Place bowl over a larger bowl filled with ice cubes and water. Using an electric mixer, whip cream at medium speed until stiff peaks form but cream is still smooth.

4. To assemble Swiss roll, turn cooled sponge onto a clean work surface. Peel off parchment paper from the bottom of sponge. Spread an even layer of whipped cream over top of sponge.

5. Peel and trim ends of bananas, then place on one edge of sponge. Drizzle caramel over bananas, then gently roll up sponge starting from side with bananas.

6. Wrap with cling film and chill in the freezer to set. Slice to serve.

Nothing epitomises the word "sweet" more than this delightful combination of sticky caramel, ripe banana and soft sponge. This Swiss roll is a treat for both children and adults alike!

japanese-style strawberry cake

Makes one 18-cm cake

Sugar syrup 3 Tbsp (made using 25 g sugar and 50 g water)

Strawberries 300 g, hulled and sliced lengthwise

Whipped cream (page 60) 1 quantity

SPONGE

Pastry flour or top flour 115 g

Eggs 170 g

Castor (superfine) sugar 130 g

Glucose 15 g

Unsalted butter 30 g

Fresh whole milk 45 g

Vanilla extract 1 tsp

VANILLA CREAM

Whipping cream (35% fat) 150 g

Fresh whole milk 20 g

Castor (superfine) sugar 15 g

Vanilla extract ¹/₂ tsp

Gelatin sheets 4 g, soaked in iced water to soften

1. Preheat oven to 170°C. Line an 18-cm round cake pan with a removable base with parchment paper. Sift flour twice. Using a clean heatproof bowl, beat eggs with a whisk, then add sugar and glucose. Place bowl over a pot of simmering water and mix well.

2. When egg mixture is warm, use an electric mixer to beat on high speed until light and fluffy. Reduce speed to low and continue beating for about 1 minute.

3. Place butter, milk and vanilla in a heatproof bowl and place over a pot of simmering water. Once butter has melted, stir through to mix.

4. Add one-sixth of egg batter to butter mixture and mix well, then add butter mixture to remaining egg batter and fold through evenly. Sift flour into bowl and fold in using a spatula until batter becomes glossy.

5. Pour batter into prepared cake pan and bake for about 40 minutes or until cake springs back when lightly touched. Remove from pan and place on a wire rack in a plastic bag to cool. When cooled completely, trim crust off the top and bottom, then slice cake horizontally to get 2 layers.

6. Place 1 layer on a flat tray and brush evenly on both sides with one-third of sugar syrup. Set this and other layer aside.

7. Make vanilla cream. Whip cream in a chilled bowl until stiff peaks form. Set aside. Place milk, sugar and vanilla in a small saucepan and bring to a boil. Add softened gelatin sheets and mix well. Let milk mixture cool to about 30°C, then add to whipped cream and fold until just incorporated.

8. Spread vanilla cream onto cake layer that was brushed with sugar syrup, then top with sliced strawberries. Place second layer of cake over and press down lightly. Refrigerate for a few minutes to set.

9. Prepare whipped cream (page 60).

10. Cover chilled cake with whipped cream, using a tablespoon to make slight indents for a decorative pattern. Garnish as desired and serve immediately.

french-style strawberry cake

Makes one 18-cm cake

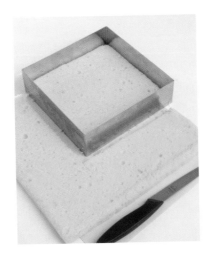

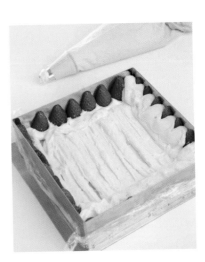

Special biscuit sponge (page 42)
1 quantity

Kirsch or cherry liqueur 1 tsp

Sugar syrup 3 Tbsp (made using 25 g sugar and 50 g water)

Strawberries 450 g, hulled and sliced lengthwise

CRÈME MOUSSELINE

Fresh whole milk 350 g

Vanilla bean 1/2, split lengthwise and scraped for seeds

Egg yolks 4

Castor (superfine) sugar 100 g

Pastry flour or top flour 35 g, sifted

Unsalted butter 200 g

Kirsch or cherry liqueur 1 Tbsp

RASPBERRY JELLY

Raspberry puree 100 g

Castor (superfine) sugar 30 g

Gelatin sheets 5 g, soaked in iced water to soften

1. Prepare special biscuit sponge (page 42).

2. When sponge is done and cooled, peel away the layer of brown skin on the top. Place an 18 x 18-cm square cake ring on cake and cut out an 18-cm square piece. Leave cake in cake ring and cover bottom of cake ring with cling film and a stainless steel tray.

3. Add kirsch or cherry liqueur to sugar syrup and brush over sponge. Set aside.

4. Make crème mousseline. Prepare a cream. Place milk and vanilla bean and seeds in a saucepan and bring to a boil. Remove from heat and set aside.

5. Whisk egg yolks with sugar until mixture is pale yellow in colour. Add flour and mix well. Discard vanilla bean.

6. Pour cream into the egg yolk mixture, then return to saucepan. Bring to a boil over high heat, stirring constantly. Continue to beat mixture until it thickens and becomes smooth and glossy. Remove from heat and transfer to a tray to cool. Cover with cling film. Place in the freezer to cool but do not freeze.

7. Beat butter with an electric mixer until creamy. Add cooled cream and beat until combined. Add kirsch or cherry liqueur and mix well. Spoon crème mousseline into a piping bag fitted with a 1-cm round piping tip.

8. Pipe a thin layer of crème mousseline onto sponge in cake ring. Arrange strawberries around edge of cake ring, with the flat surface against cake ring. Distribute remaining strawberries evenly, then pipe another layer of crème mousseline over strawberries and level with an offset spatula. Make sure there are no air pockets in cream. Place cake in the freezer for about 20 minutes.

9. Make raspberry jelly. Place raspberry purée and sugar in a small saucepan and bring to a boil. Add gelatin sheets and mix well. Pour mixture over cake and refrigerate overnight to set.

10. To unmould cake, warm sides of cake ring with a warm towel or a blowtorch. Decorate as desired. Slice and serve.

austrian coffee cream sponge cake

Makes one 30-cm cake

Blanched sliced almonds 100 g, toasted in a 150°C oven for 20 minutes

Icing (confectioner's) sugar for dusting

MERINGUE

Egg whites 2

Castor (superfine) sugar 70 g

SPONGE

Egg 1

Egg yolks 2

Castor (superfine) sugar 25 g

Pastry flour or top flour 25 g, sifted twice

COFFEE CREAM

Instant coffee granules 2 tsp

Whipping cream (35% fat) 200 g

Castor (superfine) sugar 1 Tbsp

1. Preheat oven to 160°C. Prepare a 30 x 30-cm flat square baking tray. Cut out 2 sheets of parchment paper to line tray. On one sheet, draw a straight line 4 cm from the edge of the paper and a parallel line 8-cm away. Leave a 6-cm gap and draw another 2 parallel lines 8-cm apart. Place paper in cake pan with the other sheet over it. Set aside.

2. Make meringue. Beat egg whites until foamy. Add half the sugar and continue beating for a few minutes, then add remaining sugar and beat until egg whites are glossy, with stiff peaks. Spoon meringue into a piping bag fitted with a 1.5-cm piping tip.

3. Using the first set of lines as a guide, pipe 3 strips of meringue, spacing them evenly. Repeat using the other set of lines as a guide.

4. Prepare sponge. In a heatproof mixing bowl, beat egg and egg yolks with a whisk. Add sugar, then place the bowl over a pot of boiling water and mix well. When egg mixture is warm, beat on high with an electric mixer until mixture is fluffy. Gently fold in flour with a spatula. Spoon batter into a clean piping bag fitted with a 1.5-cm piping tip.

5. Pipe batter in straight lines between the meringue strips (pictured above). Dust meringue and sponge batter strips with icing sugar twice, then place in oven to bake for 25 minutes. Once done, unmould cake and leave to cool on a wire rack.

6. Make coffee cream. Dissolve coffee granules in a bowl with a little water. Whip cream, castor sugar and coffee together in a chilled bowl until stiff peaks form.

This classic Austrian coffee cake is not difficult to do but it looks very impressive and will be the centre of attraction at any function.

7. When sponge is cool, place it on a clean work surface. Peel off the parchment paper from the bottom of the sponge.

8. Spread one piece of sponge evenly with coffee cream, then top with other piece of sponge and spread remaining coffee cream over, taking care to cover sides.

9. Coat sides of cake with sliced almonds and dust with icing sugar. Slice to serve.

chestnut cake (mont blanc)

Makes one 18-cm cake

Swiss roll sponge (page 34) 1 quantity

Whipped cream (page 60) 1 quantity

Rum 1 Tbsp

Sugar syrup 2 Tbsp (made using 25 g sugar and 50 g water)

CHESTNUTS FOR DECORATING

Chestnuts 150 g, steamed until soft, or store-bought steamed chestnuts

Castor (superfine) sugar 120 g

Water 150 g

CHESTNUT CREAM

Fresh chestnuts 200 g

Castor (superfine) sugar 40 g

Canned chestnut paste 100 g

Unsalted butter 100 g

Rum 2 tsp

WHIPPED CREAM

Whipping cream (35% fat) 200 g

Castor (superfine) sugar 2 tsp

Vanilla extract 1 tsp

1. Prepare chestnuts for decoration a day in advance. Combine steamed chestnuts, sugar and water into a small saucepan and simmer for about 15 minutes. Leave aside to cool, then chop chestnuts coarsely. Set aside.

2. Prepare Swiss roll sponge (page 34). When sponge is done, peel off brown skin from the top. Using an 18 x 18-cm round cake ring, cut out a circle, then cut out another 2 semi-circles from remaining sponge to form another 18-cm round.

3. Line the inside of a 20-cm wide plastic bowl with cling film, then place the 18-cm round sponge into the bowl, pressing it in to fit into the curvature of bowl. Mix rum and sugar syrup together, then brush one-third of mixture over sponge. Cover bowl with cling film and refrigerate until needed.

4. Make chestnut cream. Place fresh chestnuts in a saucepan and cover with water. Boil for about 15 minutes, then drain and peel off skins. Put chestnuts in a pressure cooker and add just enough water to cover. Cook for 15 minutes until soft, then drain. Alternatively, boil over the stove top until chestnuts are soft. Place chestnuts and castor sugar in a food processor and blend well. Leave aside to cool.

5. Combine cooled chestnut paste, canned chestnut paste and butter in a bowl and mix well. Add rum and fold through. Spoon chestnut cream into a piping bag fitted with a piping tip.

6. Prepare whipped cream (page 60). Combine ingredients in a clean bowl. Place bowl over a larger bowl filled with ice cubes and water. Using an electric mixer, whip cream at medium speed until stiff peaks form but cream is still smooth.

7. Spread whipped cream over soaked sponge. Sprinkle chopped chestnuts over cream, then place the 2 semi-circles of sponge over to cover cream.

8. Place an 18-cm round cake board over bowl and invert bowl to unmould cake.

9. Remove cling wrap. Spoon chestnut cream into a piping bag fitted with a 1-cm star, ribbon or Mont Blanc tip. Pipe chestnut cream over cake and decorate as desired. Slice and serve immediately.

birthday cake

Makes one 16-cm cake

Soufflé roll sponge (page 36) 1 quantity

Whipped cream (page 60) 1 quantity

Buttercream (page 58) 1 quantity

Sugar syrup 3 Tbsp (made using 25 g sugar and 50 g water)

Orange liqueur 1 Tbsp

LEMON CURD CREAM

Eggs 2

Egg yolks 2

Castor (superfine) sugar 100 g

Corn flour (cornstarch) 10 g

Lemon juice 80 g

Lemons 2, grated for zest

1. Prepare soufflé roll sponge (page 36), whipped cream (page 60) and buttercream (page 58). Keep buttercream refrigerated until needed.

2. Prepare lemon curd cream. Place eggs, egg yolks, sugar and corn flour in a small saucepan and mix well. Stir in lemon juice and lemon zest. Cook mixture over low heat while stirring constantly with a whisk until mixture thickens. Do not over-cook or mixture will become lumpy. Remove from heat and leave aside to cool.

3. To assemble cake, turn soufflé roll sponge onto a clean work surface. Peel off parchment paper from the bottom of the sponge and peel off the brown skin from the top. Cut sponge into 4 rectangular pieces.

4. Mix sugar syrup and orange liqueur and brush over sponge pieces. Spread lemon curd cream evenly over top of sponge, then cover with whipped cream.

5. Roll one length of sponge up like you would a Swiss roll. Turn cake so it stands on a cut edge. Place it on a 20-cm round cake board. With the creamed side facing in, position the second length of sponge around the first. Repeat with the third and fourth lengths of sponge until you get a round cake. Trim a little off the outermost sponge layer so that it tapers to the round shape of the cake. Smoothen any excess cream on top of cake using a spatula. Place cake in the freezer to chill and set.

6. Once set, cover cake with buttercream and decorate with piping and buttercream flowers (page 118).

BUTTERCREAM ICING

Buttercream (page 58) 2 quantities

Red, blue, yellow and green food colouring

EQUIPMENT

Five piping bags

Waxed paper

Flower nail

Petal decorating tip 102

Petal decorating tip 104

Leaf tip 70

Round tip 4

1. Divide buttercream into 5 equal portions. Colour each portion a different colour by mixing with a few drops of colouring.

2. Pipe daisies with tip 104. Use plain buttercream for petals. Place a piece of waxed paper on flower nail. Hold piping bag at a 45° angle, wide end of tip 0.5 cm away from centre of nail, with narrow part of tip pointing towards outer edge. Dot centre with a little buttercream as a guide. Starting from any point near the outer edge of nail, pipe 10 petals, squeezing and moving tip towards flower centre. Towards the centre, stop pressure and pull tip away. Change to a small round piping tip to pipe flower centre with yellow buttercream.

3. Pipe 5-petal flowers with tip 102 for smaller flowers, and 104 for bigger flowers. Use pink, blue and yellow buttercream. Place a piece of waxed paper on flower nail. Hold piping bag at a 45° angle, wide end of tip pointed away from paper and slightly to the left. Move piping tip forth and back again while twisting slightly to the right to create a ruffled petal. Make 5 petals, each petal overlapping slightly. Rotate flower nail as you pipe. Use tip 4 to pipe flower centre.

4. Pipe leaves with tip 70. Use green butter cream. Place a piece of waxed paper on flower nail. Hold piping bag at a 45° angle. Lightly touch surface of paper with wide end parallel to surface. Squeeze hard to pipe base of leaf while lifting tip slightly at the same time. Relax pressure as you pull tip towards you, forming leaf tip. Stop squeezing and lift tip away.

5. Place flowers and leaves in the freezer to chill until firm.

6. Use tip 4 or any round piping tip of desired size to pipe decorative lines on cake in alternating colours. Arrange flowers in desired fashion on cake.

pine nut tart

Makes one 22-cm tart

Sweet shortcrust pastry crust (page 50) 1 quantity

Raspberry jam 100 g

FILLING

Castor (superfine) sugar 50 g

Ground almonds 30 g

Egg 1

Egg yolk 1

Double (heavy) cream (45% fat) 140 g

Vanilla extract ¹/₂ tsp

Pine nuts 70 g

1. Prepare sweet short pastry crust (page 50).

2. Prepare filling. Mix sugar and ground almonds together. Add egg, egg yolk, cream and vanilla and mix just until incorporated. Do not over-mix.

3. Preheat oven to 180°C.

4. Spread raspberry jam over base of tart crust. Pour filling in, then sprinkle pine nuts evenly on top. Bake for 30–40 minutes until tart is golden brown in colour. Remove from heat and leave to cool on a wire rack.

5. Dust with icing sugar, if desired, and slice to serve.

fruit tart

Makes one 20-cm tart

Shortcrust pastry crust (page 48) 1 quantity

Pastry cream (page 54) 1 quantity

Whipping cream (35% fat) 40 g

Cherry or orange liqueur 1 Tbsp

Fresh fruit (strawberries, nectarines, blueberries, raspberries and mangoes)

1. Prepare shortcrust pastry crust (page 48) and pastry cream (page 54).

2. In a chilled bowl, whip whipping cream until stiff peaks form. Add whipped cream and cherry or orange liqueur to pastry cream and mix well.

3. Fill baked tart shell with pastry cream and arrange fruit on top. Dust with icing sugar just before serving. Garnish as desired.

The combination of fresh fruit and luscious cream on a crisp, buttery tart shell is indescribably delicious!

caramel nut tartlets

Makes 10 tartlets

SWEET SHORTCRUST PASTRY

Unsalted butter 140 g, at room temperature and softened

Icing (confectioner's) sugar 70 g

Salt a pinch

Vanilla extract 2 tsp

Eggs 40 g

Ground almonds 40 g

Pastry flour or top flour 260 g, sifted

ALMOND CREAM

Unsalted butter 90 g, softened

Castor (superfine) sugar 75 g

Vanilla extract 1 tsp

Ground almonds 90 g

Eggs 75 g

CARAMEL CREAM

Castor (superfine) sugar 75 g

Glucose 10 g

Whipping cream (35% fat) 100 g

Unsalted butter 50 g

1. Prepare sweet short pastry. Beat butter, icing sugar, salt and vanilla extract with an electric mixer until just combined. Add egg yolk and beat well. Add ground almonds and mix well. Add flour and fold through completely. Using a bench scraper, mix batter until a smooth dough is formed. Wrap dough in cling film, then place in the refrigerator to rest for at least 3 hours.

2. Preheat oven to 180°C.

3. Unwrap dough and place on a non-stick baking mat or parchment paper. Roll out to a thickness of 3–5 mm.

4. Using a 9.5-cm fluted pastry cutter, cut out 10 rounds from pastry. Gently press cut dough into 10 round tartlet tins, each 8 x 3-cm. Prick centres with a fork. Chill dough in the freezer for about 10 minutes, then bake for 20 minutes or until tart shells are light golden brown. Remove from heat and set aside to cool. Keep oven heated.

5. Prepare almond cream. Beat butter and sugar until just combined. Add vanilla and mix. Add ground almonds, followed by eggs and mix well. Do not over-mix. Spoon almond cream into a piping bag fitted with a 1-cm piping tip and pipe cream into tart shells, filling them up only halfway. Bake for 20 minutes until golden brown in colour.

6. Prepare caramel cream. Place sugar and glucose in a saucepan and heat until sugar caramelises. Gradually add cream while stirring with a spatula. Mix until smooth. Remove from heat and leave to cool slightly. Add unsalted butter.

ASSORTED NUTS

Hazelnuts 20 g

Almond slivers 20 g

Walnuts 20 g

Pistachios 20 g

DRIED FRUIT

Dried apricots 6

Dried figs 3

Black raisins 30 g

Dried cranberries 30 g

7. Bake assorted nuts in the oven for 20 minutes at 150°C without preheating oven.

8. Blanch dried fruit in boiling water, then drain and pat-dry. Cut blanched dried fruit into small cubes. Stir toasted nuts and dried fruit into caramel cream. Spoon mixture onto prepared tart shells and serve.

apple and mincemeat tartlets

Makes 12 tartlets

SHORTCRUST PASTRY

Cold unsalted butter 120 g, cut into small cubes

Pastry flour or top flour 200 g

Castor (superfine) sugar 1/2 tsp

Salt 1/2 tsp

Ice-cold water 100 g

APPLE FILLING

Unsalted butter 10 g

Green apples 2, peeled, cored and thinly sliced

Castor (superfine) sugar 1 Tbsp

Store-bought mincemeat mixture 100 g

Icing (confectioner's) sugar for dusting

ALMOND MIXTURE

Eggs 2

Castor (superfine) sugar 80 g

Sour cream 50 g

Double (heavy) cream (45% fat) 50 g

Ground almonds 50 g

Unsalted butter 60 g, melted

1. Prepare shortcrust pastry 2 days in advance. Combine butter cubes and flour in a plastic bag. Place in the freezer overnight.

2. Using a food processor, pulse butter and flour mixture, sugar and salt until the mixture resembles coarse breadcrumbs. Add water and mix until a smooth dough is formed. Place dough on a floured surface and knead lightly. Leave dough to rest in the refrigerator overnight.

3. On the day of baking, place dough on a non-stick baking mat or parchment paper and roll out to a thickness of 5 mm. Use a 9.5-cm fluted round pastry cutter to cut out 12 rounds from pastry. Gently press cut dough into 12 round tartlet tins, each 6.5 x 2-cm. Prick centres with a fork. Chill dough in the freezer for about 10 minutes

4. Make apple filling. Combine butter, apples and sugar in a small saucepan and cook over medium heat until apple slices are golden brown in colour. Add mincemeat mixture and mix well. Transfer filling to a tray and leave aside to cool. When cool, spoon filling into tart shells.

5. Make almond mixture. Lightly beat eggs and sugar together. Add sour cream, double cream, ground almonds and melted butter and mix thoroughly. Pour mixture over apple filling, then dust with icing sugar.

6. Preheat oven to 200°C. Bake tartlets for 20 minutes, then reduce temperature to 180°C and continue bake for another 15 minutes. Remove from heat and leave to cool slightly on a wire rack.

7. Dust tartlets with icing sugar and serve warm.

This traditional, well-loved favourite is best eaten freshly baked as the sweet tartness of the fruit and mincemeat filling contrasts perfectly with the warm, buttery pastry.

orange almond butter cake

Makes one 18-cm cake

Blanched and sliced almond as needed

Eggs 2

Egg yolk 1

Ground almonds 85 g

Icing (confectioner's) sugar 90 g

Pastry flour or top flour 25 g, sifted

Candied orange peel 70 g, cut into small
pieces

Unsalted butter 35 g, melted

Apricot jam 100 g

Water 1 tsp

SUGAR GLAZE
Icing (confectioner's) sugar 90 g

Lemon juice 20 g

1. Preheat oven to 170°C. Lightly grease an 18-cm round cake pan with some softened butter. Spread sliced almonds evenly over base of cake pan.

2. Combine eggs and egg yolk and beat lightly. In a separate bowl, combine ground almonds and icing sugar and stir lightly. Add one-third of egg mixture to almond mixture and beat with an electric mixer. Repeat another two times until the mixture is light, fluffy and pale. Do not over-beat.

3. Add flour and candied orange peel to egg and almond mixture and fold in well. Add melted butter and fold in thoroughly.

4. Pour batter into prepared cake pan and bake for about 40 minutes. Unmould cake from pan and leave to cool on a wire rack.

5. Combine apricot jam and water in a small bowl and mix well. Heat lightly in the microwave oven for about 30 seconds, then brush liberally over cake.

6. Make sugar glaze. Combine icing sugar and lemon juice in a bowl and mix well. Brush over cake. Decorate cake as desired.

7. Leave sugar glaze to dry before slicing cake to serve.

earl grey tea cake

Makes one 19-cm loaf

Pastry flour or top flour 150 g, softened

Baking powder 1/8 tsp

Sugar syrup 100 g (made using 50 g sugar and 100 g water)

Lemon juice 2 Tbsp

Unsalted butter 150 g, softened

Icing (confectioner's) sugar 150 g

Glucose 15 g

Eggs 150 g, about 3 eggs

Salt 1/8 tsp

Earl grey tea dust from tea bags 5 g

Ground almonds 15 g

Lemon 1, grated for zest

Fresh whole milk 1 Tbsp

1. Preheat oven to 170°C. Line a 19 x 9 x 8-cm loaf tin with parchment paper. Sift flour and baking powder together twice.

2. Mix sugar syrup with lemon juice. Set aside.

3. Beat butter, icing sugar and glucose together until light and very fluffy. Gradually add eggs and beat well, then add salt, tea dust, ground almonds. lemon zest and milk. Mix well.

4. Add flour mixture and fold through completely using a spatula. Surface of batter should be glossy and smooth.

5. Pour batter into prepared loaf tin and make a lengthwise 'cut' down the middle of batter with a spatula. Bake for about 50 minutes. Note that the baking time may vary according to your oven.

6. When the cake is done, unmould cake and peel away parchment paper. Place cake on a wire rack set over a tray and brush with sugar and lemon syrup while cake is still warm.

7. Leave to cool completely before serving. If storing, wrap with cling film.

Refer to the recipe for pound cake (page 52) for more tips and instructions.

Sometimes, all you really need is a simple, no-fuss cake like this pound cake which goes perfectly with coffee or tea.

rum fruit cake

Makes one 21-cm loaf

MIXED FRUIT IN RUM

Dried prunes 100 g

Dried apricots 100 g

Dried figs 10 pieces

Raisins 300 g

Sultanas 100 g

Dried cranberries 100 g

Candied orange 100 g

Candied cherries 100 g

Cinnamon sticks 2

Rum 400 g

Brandy 300 g

Red wine 100 g

FRUIT CAKE

Pastry flour or top flour 150 g

Baking powder 1/2 tsp

Rum 5 Tbsp

Sugar syrup 4 Tbsp (made using 50 g
    sugar and 100 g water)

Store-bought mincemeat mixture
    150 g

Unsalted butter 120 g, softened

1. Prepare mixed fruit in rum at least 2 weeks in advance. Poach all dried fruit in a pot of boiling water, then strain. In a pan and without using any oil, dry-fry fruit until dry.

2. Cut prunes, apricots and figs into small pieces, then return to dried fruit mixture. Transfer fruit mixture to a big jar with a lid, then add cinnamon sticks, rum, brandy and red wine. Seal jar tightly and leave mixture for at least 2 weeks. Mixed fruit in rum can be stored at room temperature for up to 1 year.

3. To make cake, preheat oven to 170°C. Line a 21 x 10 x 7.5-cm loaf tin with parchment paper. Sift flour and baking powder together twice.

4. Make a rum syrup by mixing rum with sugar syrup. Set aside.

5. Drain excess syrup from mixed fruit. Pat fruit dry with paper towels to remove excess moisture, then combine with mincemeat. Set aside.

6. Beat butter, brown sugar, ground ginger, cinnamon, allspice and nutmeg until light and very fluffy. Gradually add eggs and beat well, then add molasses and ground almonds. Add flour, mixed fruit and mincemeat mixture and fold to combine.

7. Pour batter into prepared loaf tin and make a lengthwise 'cut' down the middle of batter with a spatula. Bake for about 1 hour 10 minutes. Note that the baking time may vary according to your oven.

Brown sugar 120 g

Ground ginger $\frac{1}{2}$ tsp

Ground cinnamon $\frac{1}{2}$ tsp

Ground allspice $\frac{1}{4}$ tsp

Ground nutmeg $\frac{1}{8}$ tsp

Eggs 2

Molasses 1 Tbsp

Ground almonds 20 g

8. When cake is done, unmould cake and peel away parchment paper. Place cake on a wire rack set over a tray and brush with rum syrup while cake is still warm.

9. Leave to cool completely before serving. If storing, wrap with cling film.

Refer to the recipe for pound cake (page 52) for more tips and instructions.

chocolate cake

Makes one 18-cm cake

Pastry flour or top flour 35 g

Cocoa powder 50 g

Sweet chocolate (55% cocoa) 100 g, cut into small cubes

Unsalted butter 80 g, cut into small cubes

Castor (superfine) sugar 40 g

Egg yolks 4

Whipping cream (35% fat) 50 g

MERINGUE

Egg whites 4

Castor (superfine) sugar 100 g

WHIPPED CREAM

Whipping cream (35% fat) 200 g

Castor (superfine) sugar 2 tsp

1. Preheat oven to 170°C. Prepare an 18-cm round cake pan with a removable base. Line with parchment paper. Sift flour and cocoa powder together twice.

2. Melt chocolate and butter in a heatproof bowl set over a pot of simmering water. Once chocolate and butter have melted, add sugar, egg yolks and cream and mix well using a whisk. Set aside.

3. Make meringue. Beat egg whites until foamy. Add half the sugar and continue beating for a few minutes, then add remaining sugar and beat until egg whites are glossy and stiff peaks form.

4. Add one-third of meringue to chocolate mixture and fold with a whisk. Add flour and cocoa powder and fold in thoroughly. Add remaining meringue and fold just until incorporated.

5. Pour batter into prepared cake pan and bake for about 50 minutes. Note that the baking time may vary according to your oven. When cake is done, unmould from pan and leave to cool on a wire rack.

6. Make whipped cream (page 60). Combine ingredients in a clean bowl. Place bowl over a larger bowl filled with ice cubes and water. Using an electric mixer, whip cream at medium speed until stiff peaks form but cream is still smooth.

7. Dust cake with icing sugar. Slice and serve with whipped cream. Garnish as desired.

Chocolate never fails to satisfy the palate, and this chocolate cake will not fail to please your guests and family when it is time for dessert!

super vanilla cheesecake

Makes one 15-cm cheesecake

Wheat crackers 65 g

Unsalted butter 25 g, melted

Cream cheese 220 g

Castor (superfine) sugar 50 g

Egg yolks 2

Whipping cream (35% fat) 1 Tbsp

Vanilla extract 1 tsp, or 1 vanilla bean,
 split lengthwise and scraped for seeds

Canned blueberries 60 g, drained and
 pat-dry with paper towels to remove
 excess moisture

Sour cream 130 g

Icing (confectioner's) sugar 20 g

1. Make cheesecake a day in advance. Preheat oven to 170°C. Prepare a 15-cm round cake pan with a removable base. Lightly grease with softened butter.

2. Place wheat crackers in a food processor and lightly pulse into fine crumbs. Add melted butter and mix well.

3. Transfer crumbs to cake pan and spread evenly. Press down to pack crumbs tightly together, using the base of a glass cup, then place pan in the refrigerator to set.

4. Place cream cheese in the microwave oven and heat at 600w (Medium) for about 15 seconds or until softened. Place in a food processor together with sugar, egg yolks, cream and vanilla and blend well.

5. Arrange blueberries over cracker base, then pour cream cheese mixture over and bake for 20–25 minutes until top of cheesecake is light brown and the centre feels springy to the touch. Remove cheesecake from oven.

6. Increase oven temperature to 200°C.

7. Mix together sour cream and icing sugar. Heat in the microwave oven at 600w (Medium) for about 30 seconds until mixture becomes fluid. Pour over baked cheesecake and return to the oven to bake for another 2 minutes for sour cream layer to set.

8. Remove cheesecake from oven and leave to cool on a wire rack. Cover with cling film and refrigerate overnight.

9. To unmould cheesecake, warm sides of cake pan with a warm towel or a blowtorch. To slice cake, use a warm knife. Garnish as desired. Serve immediately.

pineapple yoghurt cheesecake

Makes one 18-cm square cake

Special biscuit sponge (page 42)
1 quantity

Orange liqueur ¹/₂ tsp

Sugar syrup 2 Tbsp (made using 25 g sugar and 50 g water)

HOMEMADE PINEAPPLE COMPOTE

Pineapple 1

Water 300 g

Castor (superfine) sugar 150 g

Orange liqueur 1 Tbsp

YOGHURT CREAM CHEESE

Cream cheese 200 g

Castor (superfine) sugar 80 g

Sugar-free plain yoghurt 300 g

Whipping cream (35% fat) 100 g

Lemon juice 1 Tbsp

Orange liqueur 1 Tbsp

Gelatin sheets 5 g, soaked in iced water to soften

1. Prepare homemade pineapple compote a day in advance. Peel pineapple, then cut into small pieces. Combine water and sugar in a saucepan and bring to a boil. Once mixture boils, turn off heat and add liqueur. Add pineapple pieces to the hot syrup and cover saucepan with cling film. Leave mixture to rest overnight. To skip this step, use 130 g canned pineapple, cut into small cubes.

2. Make cheesecake a day in advance. Prepare special biscuit sponge (page 42).

3. Peel off brown skin from the top of sponge. Using an 18 x 18-cm square cake ring, cut out an 18-cm square from biscuit sponge. Leave cake in cake ring and place on a stainless steel tray or cake board.

4. Combine orange liqueur and sugar syrup, then brush over cake. Set aside.

5. Make yoghurt cream cheese. Beat cream cheese and castor sugar with an electric mixer until creamy. Add yoghurt, cream, lemon juice and orange liqueur and blend together.

6. Place softened gelatin sheets in a heatproof bowl and heat gently over a pot of simmering water. Once gelatin has melted, add to cream cheese mixture and mix until incorporated.

7. Transfer half the yoghurt cream cheese into another bowl. Add pineapple compote or canned pineapple and fold together. Pour mixture over sponge, then level evenly with an offset spatula. Pour remaining yoghurt cream cheese over and level again. Refrigerate overnight to set.

8. To unmould cake, warm sides of cake pan with a warm towel or a blowtorch. To slice cake, use a warm knife. Garnish as desired. Serve immediately.

The use of yoghurt makes this cheesecake lighter than traditional cheesecakes, and really sets off the pineapple flavour!

keiko-style mango pudding

Serves 7

Fresh whole milk 250 g

Castor (superfine) sugar 50 g

Egg yolks 2

Gelatin sheets 5 g, soaked in ice water to
   softened

Mango purée 150 g

Mango 150 g, peeled and diced

Whipped cream (page 60) 80 g

1. Make a custard sauce. Combine milk and half the sugar in a saucepan and bring to a boil. Beat egg yolks and the remaining sugar until a light emulsion is formed. Add half the hot milk mixture to egg yolk mixture and mix well. Add to contents in saucepan and stir over low heat until mixture thickens. Add gelatin and mix through.

2. Strain mixture, then add mango purée and diced mango. Cool mango cream quickly by placing bowl in another bowl filled with iced water.

3. Fold whipped cream into chilled mango cream. Pour into serving glasses. Refrigerate for at least 3 hours until set and well-chilled before serving. Garnish as desired.

almond snow balls

Makes about 45 cookies

Pastry flour or top flour 150 g

Unsalted butter 120 g, softened

Icing (confectioner's) sugar 50 g +
more for dusting

Salt a pinch

Vanilla extract ¹/₂ tsp

Ground almonds 50 g

1. Preheat oven to 160°C. Sift flour once. Line a baking tray with parchment paper.

2. Beat butter, sugar, salt and vanilla until softened. Fold flour and ground almonds into butter mixture using a spatula or scraper. Wrap dough with cling film and refrigerate for about 20 minutes.

3. Roll chilled dough into a long cylinder about 3-cm in diameter. Slice roll and weigh the pieces to check that they are uniform in size, about 8 g each.

4. Shape dough pieces into balls and place in alternating rows on prepared baking tray to ensure good distribution of oven heat for even baking.

5. Bake cookies for 20 minutes, then remove from heat and leave to cool on a wire rack.

6. Once cooled, dust cookies with icing sugar and store in an airtight container to keep them crisp.

chocolate almond cookies

Makes about 40 cookies

Sliced and blanched almonds 40 g

Pastry flour or top flour 150 g

Cocoa powder 20 g

Unsalted butter 120 g, softened

Icing (confectioner's) sugar 70 g

Salt a pinch

Egg yolk 1

Granulated white sugar for dusting

1. Preheat oven to 150°C. Place almonds on a baking tray and bake for 20 minutes. Sift flour and cocoa powder together once.

2. Beat butter, icing sugar and salt until softened. Add egg yolk and mix well.

3. Fold flour and cocoa powder mixture into butter mixture using a spatula. Add toasted almond slivers and fold through. Cover dough with cling wrap and refrigerate for about 15 minutes.

4. Divide cookie dough into two portions. Place each portion on a sheet of parchment paper and shape it into logs about 4-cm in diameter. Wrap logs with parchment paper and refrigerate. If not baking cookies immediately, wrap logs again in cling film and freeze for up to 2 months.

5. Preheat oven to 160°C.

6. Slice cookie dough log into 7-mm thick pieces. Roll side of cookies in granulated sugar and place on a baking tray lined with parchment paper or a non-stick baking mat. Bake for about 20 minutes. Remove from heat and leave to cool on a wire rack.

7. Serve or store cookies in an airtight container at room temperature for up to 10 days.

blueberry crumble muffins

Makes 6 muffins

CRUMBLE TOPPING

Cold unsalted butter 20 g

Castor (superfine) sugar 20 g

Pastry flour or top flour 20 g, sifted

Ground almonds 10 g

MUFFINS

Pastry flour or top flour 120 g

Baking powder 1 tsp

Fresh blueberries 100 g

Unsalted butter 50 g, softened

Brown sugar 40 g

Castor (superfine) sugar 30 g

Egg 65 g, abut 1 egg

Cold fresh whole milk 60 g

1. Make crumble topping. Combine ingredients in a bowl and mix with fingers until mixture resembles coarse breadcrumbs. Refrigerate until needed.

2. Preheat oven to 180°C. Sift flour and baking powder together twice. Set aside 18 blueberries.

3. Beat butter with an electric handheld mixer until soft and creamy. Add both sugars and beat until mixture is light and fluffy. Add egg and beat until well-combined.

4. Add one-third of flour and fold in with a spatula. Add half the milk and continue to fold batter gently. Add another one-third of flour and fold in, followed by the remaining milk. Add remaining flour and fold through but do not over-mix. Add remaining blueberries and fold in gently.

5. Line a 6-hole muffin tray with paper cases. Spoon batter into cases until about three-quarters full. Top each muffin with 3 blueberries, then sprinkle crumble topping over. Bake for 25–30 minutes or until muffins spring back with gently touched.

6. Leave muffins to cool on a wire rack. They are best served warm and consumed within 1–2 days. If not consuming immediately, store in an airtight container and refrigerate for up to 4 days or freeze for up to 2 weeks.

TIPS

To reheat muffins using a microwave oven, heat thawed muffins for 30 seconds and frozen muffins for 1½–2 minutes at 500w (Medium).

To reheat muffins using an oven, preheat the oven to 180°C. Heat thawed muffins for 5 minutes and frozen muffins for 8–10 minutes.

To reheat muffins using a toaster oven, wrap the muffins with aluminium foil. Heat thawed muffins for 5–6 minutes and frozen muffins for 10–12 minutes.

scones with homemade jam

Makes about 10 scones

SCONES

Pastry flour or top flour 220 g or replace 170 g pastry or top flour with 50 g wholemeal flour to make wholemeal scones

Baking powder 1 Tbsp

Cold unsalted butter 80 g, cut into small cubes

Castor (superfine) sugar 30 g

Salt 1/2 tsp

Egg yolk and milk mixture 110 g (combine 1 egg yolk with enough fresh whole milk to make up amount)

Raisins 40 g (optional)

APRICOT JAM

Dried apricots 200 g

Water 300 g

Castor (superfine) sugar 200 g

Lemon juice from half a lemon

YUZU JAM

Yuzu fruit 3 (about 240–300 g)

Water 200 g

Castor (superfine) sugar 120–150 g

Lemon juice 1 Tbsp

PLUM JAM

Fresh red plums 500 g

Castor (superfine) sugar 250 g

Lemon juice from 1 lemon

1. Prepare flour and butter a day in advance. Sift flour and baking powder together. Place butter and flour together in a plastic bag and refrigerate overnight.

2. On the day of baking, preheat oven to 200°C. Pulse butter-flour mixture together with sugar and salt in a food processor until mixture resembles coarse breadcrumbs. Add egg yolk and milk mixture and mix until a smooth dough is formed. If using raisins, add at this point together with milk and egg yolk mixture.

3. To make scones without a food processor, combine flour, sugar and salt in a bowl. Add butter and use your fingertips to rub flour into butter until mixture resembles coarse breadcrumbs. Add milk and egg yolk mixture and mix with a scraper. If using raisins, add at this point together with milk and egg yolk mixture.

4. Place dough on a floured surface and knead lightly. Roll out to a thickness of 1.5–2 cm. Dust a 5-cm round pastry cutter with flour, then cut out as many rounds of dough as possible.

5. Place rounds on a baking tray and brush with milk. Bake for 12–15 minutes until scones are golden brown. Remove from heat and cool on a wire rack. Serve scones warm, with jam of choice and cream on the side.

HOMEMADE JAMS

These homemade jams will keep refrigerated up to a year if they remain sealed, and up to 1 month after opening. To clean and sterilise jam jars, place jars and their lids in a big pot and pour in enough water to cover. Boil for 30 minutes, then remove jars and lids carefully with tongs and wipe dry.

APRICOT JAM

1. Combine apricots and water in a small saucepan. Cook for 5 minutes over medium heat, then turn off heat. Leave to sit until apricots plump up.

2. Place softened apricots in a food processor and blend into a smooth paste. Transfer paste to a small pan and add sugar and lemon juice. Let mixture simmer gently over 10 minutes over low heat, stirring occasionally. Fill sterilised jam jars with hot jam and seal tightly.

YUZU JAM

1. Cut yuzu fruit in half. Squeeze for juice and slice peel thinly. Weigh yuzu peel and juice, then weigh out an amount of sugar that is half the weight of the yuzu peel and juice.

2. Place yuzu peel in a small pan and pour in enough water to barely cover. Bring to a boil and drain peel, then rinse under running water. Repeat this step twice.

3. Place cooked yuzu peel, juice, water, sugar and lemon juice in a pan and simmer for 15 minutes over low heat, stirring occasionally. Fill sterilised jam jars with hot jam and seal tightly.

PLUM JAM

1. Deseed plums and place in a saucepan. Add sugar and lemon juice and bring to a boil, skimming off any scum that floats to the surface.

2. Reduce heat and leave to simmer for about 40 minutes over low heat, stirring occasionally, until volume has reduced by one-third. Fill sterilised jam jars with hot jam and seal tightly.

chocolate puffy macarons

Makes about 15 macarons

CHOCOLATE MACARONS

Pastry flour or top flour 5 g

Ground almonds 70 g

Icing (confectioner's) sugar 75 g

Cocoa powder 20 g

Castor (superfine) sugar 30 g

Egg white powder 4 g

Egg whites 100 g

CHOCOLATE GANACHE

Whipping cream (35% fat) 50 g

Sweet chocolate (55% cocoa) 50 g, chopped

Unsalted butter 5 g, softened

1. Preheat oven to 160°C. Line a baking tray with parchment paper. Sift together flour, ground almonds, icing sugar and cocoa powder twice with a coarse sieve.

2. Make a meringue. Combine castor sugar and egg white powder together. Beat egg whites until foamy. Add sugar and egg white powder mixture and beat until egg whites are glossy and stiff peaks form. Add flour mixture to meringue and fold in lightly.

3. Spoon batter into a piping bag fitted with a 1-cm piping tip. Pipe batter in small rounds (about 3.5-cm in diameter) onto lined baking tray. Dust with icing sugar twice, then bake for about 15 minutes. Remove from heat and set aside to cool on a baking tray.

4. Make chocolate ganache. Bring cream to a boil in a saucepan over medium heat. Once cream boils, remove from heat. Place chocolate in a bowl and pour hot cream over. Let mixture sit for 30 seconds, then stir with a spatula until smooth. Add butter and mix well. Set aside to cool.

5. Spoon chocolate ganache into a clean piping bag fitted with a 1-cm piping tip. Pipe chocolate ganache onto the flat side of half the chocolate macarons. Sandwich with remaining chocolate macarons.

6. These macarons are best made a day in advance and left to chill in the refrigerator before serving. To store, keep in an airtight container and refrigerate for up to 7 days.

special recipes
(free of eggs, dairy, gelatin and refined sugar)

red fruit jelly

Serves 8

Strawberries 10

Water 270 g

Agar-agar powder 4 g

Sugar-free grape juice 2 Tbsp

Lemon juice 2 Tbsp

Agave syrup 60 g

Raspberries 15

Blueberries 20

Red currants 6 tsp

Blackberries 8

1. Wash and hull strawberries, then cut into small pieces. Set aside.

2. Combine water and agar-agar powder in a small saucepan and bring to a boil, stirring constantly. Add grape juice, lemon juice and agave syrup and stir well. Remove from heat and leave jelly mixture to cool slightly.

3. Place fruit into a glass serving bowl, then pour jelly mixture over. Refrigerate to chill and set before serving.

carrot, ginger, rum & raisin cake

Makes one 24-cm loaf

Raisins 60 g

Rum 2 Tbsp

Walnuts 40 g

Unbleached plain (all-purpose) flour
    180 g, sifted

Aluminium-free baking powder $1/2$ Tbsp

Ground cinnamon $1/2$ tsp

Ground ginger 1 tsp

Maple syrup 140 g

Beet sugar 60 g

Safflower oil 60 g

Carrots 150 g, peeled and coarsely
    grated

Ground almonds 140 g

1. Prepare raisins a day in advance. Poach raisins in a small saucepan of boiling water for 1 minute and drain well. Leave raisins to soak in rum overnight.

2. Without preheating oven, toast walnuts at 150°C for 15–20 minutes. Leave to cool, then chop into small pieces.

3. Preheat oven to 170°C. Line a 24 x 8 x 6-cm loaf tin with parchment paper. Sift flour, baking powder, ground cinnamon and ginger together twice.

4. Combine maple syrup, beet sugar and safflower oil in a bowl and stir to combine. Add carrots and fold in. Add flour, ground almonds, rum-soaked raisins and toasted walnuts into the bowl and fold in with a spatula.

5. Pour batter into prepared loaf tin and make a lengthwise 'cut' down the middle of batter with a spatula. Bake for about 50 minutes. Note that the baking time may vary according to your oven.

6. When cake is done, turn it out onto a clean work surface. Peel off the parchment paper from the bottom of cake and leave to cool on a wire rack. When cake is cool, wrap with cling film and keep for at least 2 days before serving. The flavour of the cake improves with age.

strawberry soy cream cake

Makes one 28-cm cake

Strawberries 250 g, washed, hulled and sliced lengthwise

Sugar-free apple juice 3 Tbsp

SPONGE

Maple syrup 55 g

Brown rice syrup 50 g

Sea salt 1/2 tsp

Sticky Chinese yam 70 g, grated

Soy milk 160 g

Safflower or grapeseed oil 55 g

Unbleached plain (all-purpose) flour 100 g, sifted twice

Brown rice flour 70 g, sifted twice

Ground hazelnuts 20 g

Aluminium-free baking powder 1 tsp

SOY CREAM

Sugar-free apple juice 150 g

Agar-agar powder 1/2 tsp

Firm bean curd 400 g, drained and pat dry with paper towels

Agave syrup 80 g

Vanilla extract 1 tsp

Lemon 1, grated for zest

1. Preheat oven to 170°C. Line a 20 x 20-cm square cake pan with parchment paper.

2. Make sponge. Place maple syrup, brown rice syrup, salt and yam in a bowl and beat well. Add soy milk and oil and mix well. Add plain flour, brown rice flour, ground hazelnuts and baking powder and fold well with a spatula.

3. Pour batter into prepared cake pan and spread evenly with a scraper. Place cake pan on a baking tray and bake for about 25 minutes. Unmould sponge and place in a plastic bag to cool.

4. Turn cooled sponge out onto a clean work surface and peel off parchment paper. Slice sponge into 3 rectangular pieces, then slice one piece across into half. Set aside.

5. Make soy cream. Combine apple juice and agar-agar powder in a small saucepan and heat, stirring continuously, until agar-agar powder is completely melted. Remove from heat and set aside.

6. Place bean curd, agave syrup, vanilla and lemon zest into a food processor and blend well. Add agar-agar mixture and blend thoroughly.

7. To assemble cake, place one rectangular sponge piece on a long serving plate. Lengthen it with one-half of the halved cake.

8. Brush apple juice over sponge, then spread with one-quarter of soycream. Top with sliced strawberries, then spread another one-quarter of soy cream over strawberries. Sandwich with remaining sponge slices and spread remaining soy cream over the top and sides of cake.

9. Decorate as desired. Slice and serve.

My friends and family find it hard to believe that this cake is low-fat and healthy! I love how the bean curd cream lends a rich creaminess to this cake without being heavy and satiating.

sweet potato cupcakes

Makes 7–8 cupcakes

Japanese sweet potato 170 g,
    scrubbed clean

Beet sugar 50 g + 2 Tbsp

Unbleached plain (all-purpose) flour
    90 g, sifted

Wholemeal flour 40 g, sifted

Aluminium-free baking powder 1 Tbsp

Sea salt 1/8 tsp

Sticky Chinese yam 60 g, grated

Soy milk 120 g

Vanilla extract 1 tsp

Safflower or grapeseed oil 20 g

Raisins 30 g

1. Line 7–8 muffin or pudding cups with paper cases. Set aside.

2. Cut sweet potato into small cubes. Place in a small saucepan and add 2 Tbsp beet sugar. Pour in just enough water to cover. Simmer until sweet potatoes soften, then drain and set aside.

3. Sift both flours and baking powder together.

4. Place remaining beet sugar, sea salt and yam in a bowl and beat well. Add soy milk, vanilla extract and safflower or grapeseed oil and mix well. Add flour mixture and fold in well with a spatula. Add half the cooked sweet potatoes and raisins to batter and fold in.

5. Pour batter into prepared paper cases. Top each muffin with remaining pieces of sweet potato. Heat water in a steamer until boiling, then steam cupcakes over high heat for 20 minutes or until well risen. Remove from steamer and leave to cool on a wire rack.

6. Serve cupcakes warm or at room temperature.

These simple cupcakes are a favourite treat in Japanese households, and they are so easy to make!

green tea cookies

Makes about 20 cookies

Unbleached plain (all-purpose) flour 100 g, sifted

Baking powder a pinch, sifted

Green tea powder 5 g, sifted

Ground almonds 50 g, sifted

Brown rice syrup 15 g

Maple syrup 45 g

Sea salt a pinch

Safflower or grapeseed oil 25 g

1. Preheat oven to 150°C. Sift flour, baking powder, green tea powder and ground almonds twice.

2. Combine brown rice syrup, maple syrup, sea salt and oil in a bowl and mix well. Add flour mixture and fold in with a spatula, then rub dough quickly with your fingers until crumbly.

3. Sandwich dough with parchment paper or a non-stick baking mat and roll it out to a thickness of 5 mm. If dough becomes too soft, refrigerate it for a few minutes.

4. Cut cookies out with a 3.5-cm square cookie cutter or a cookie cutter of choice, then place on a baking tray lined with parchment paper. Bake cookies for 15–20 minutes or until firm. Remove from heat and leave to cool on a wire rack.

5. Store cookies in an airtight container at room temperature for up to 10 days.

hazelnut cookies

Makes about 20 cookies

Unbleached plain (all-purpose) flour
  100 g, sifted

Aluminium-free baking powder a pinch

Ground hazelnuts 50 g, sifted

Maple syrup 55 g

Sea salt a pinch

Safflower or grapeseed oil 25 g

1. Preheat oven to 160°C. Combine flour, baking powder and hazelnuts in a bowl and rub together with your fingertips.

2. Combine maple syrup, sea salt and oil in a bowl and mix well. Add flour mixture and fold in with a spatula. Rub dough quickly with your fingers until crumbly.

3. Sandwich dough with parchment paper or a non-stick baking mat and roll it out to a thickness of about 5 mm. If dough becomes too soft, refrigerate it for a few minutes.

4. Cut cookies out with a 5-cm flower-shaped cookie cutter or a cookie cutter of choice, then place on a baking tray lined with parchment paper. Bake cookies for 15–20 minutes or until firm. Remove from heat and leave to cool on a wire rack.

5. Store cookies in an airtight container at room temperature for up to 10 days.

energy bar

Makes 6 bars

Walnuts 30 g

Brown rice syrup 70 g

Sugar-free apple juice 50 g

Pine nuts 30 g

Pumpkin seeds 20 g

Raisins 50 g

Dried cranberries 20 g

Rolled oats 60 g

Wholemeal flour 60 g

1. Without preheating oven, toast walnuts at 150°C for 15 minutes. Leave to cool, then chop into small pieces and set aside.

2. Combine brown rice syrup and apple juice in a bowl and mix well. Add walnuts, pine nuts, pumpkin seeds, raisins, cranberries and oats. Mix until combined. Add flour and fold in.

3. Transfer mixture to a medium-size freezer bag (about 13 x 24-cm) and seal. Use a rolling pin to roll the mixture out to take the shape of the freezer bag. Place in freezer for 1 hour.

4. Preheat oven to 150°C. Using scissors, cut open the freezer bag. Using a knife, cut mixture into 6 bars and place on a baking tray lined with parchment paper.

5. Bake bars for about 25 minutes. Remove from heat and leave to cool on a wire rack.

6. Store bars in an airtight container.

Why bother with store-bought muesli bars when you can easily make your own? These are great for a quick snack or bite while on the go.

peanut butter cookies

Makes about 25 cookies

Unbleached plain (all-purpose) flour
  80 g

Wholemeal flour 40 g

Aluminium-free baking powder 1/8 tsp

Ground peanuts 40 g

Brown rice syrup 60 g

Maple syrup 50 g

Crunchy peanut butter 70 g

Safflower or grapeseed oil 50 g

1. Preheat oven to 160°C. Sift flours, baking powder and ground peanuts together twice. Line a baking tray with parchment paper.

2. Combine brown rice syrup, maple syrup, peanut butter and oil in a bowl and mix well. Add flour mixture and fold in with a spatula. Cookie dough should be soft and sticky.

3. Spoon 1 Tbsp cookie dough on prepared baking tray and flatten dough with a fork. Repeat until cookie dough is used up. Keep cookies slightly apart.

4. Bake cookies 15–20 minutes or until light golden brown. Remove from heat and leave to cool on a wire rack.

5. Store cookies in an airtight container at room temperature for up to 10 days.

green tea jelly with red bean paste

Serves 6–8

GREEN TEA JELLY

Kuzu powder 15 g

Room temperature water 200 g

Hot water 100 g

Green tea powder 8 g

Soy milk 200 g

Agar-agar powder 4 g

Agave syrup 90 g

RED BEAN PASTE

Red beans (*azuki*) 100 g, washed and drained

Beet sugar 50 g

Salt a pinch

1. Combine *kuzu* powder and 2 Tbsp water in a small bowl and mix well. In a separate bowl, gradually add hot water to green tea powder while stirring until completely dissolved.

2. Combine soy milk, remaining room temperature water, agar-agar powder and *kuzu* mixture in a small saucepan and bring to a full boil while stirring continuously. Add agave syrup and green tea mixture and mix well. Remove from heat and strain.

3. Pour mixture into 6–8 jelly moulds and refrigerate until set.

4. Meanwhile, make red bean paste. Wash red beans well. Boil beans in a pot of water, then drain and transfer to a saucepan.

5. Pour in enough water to cover beans, then simmer over low heat for about 1 hour until beans are soft. Skim off any scum that rises to the surface. When beans are soft, remove from heat and drain.

6. Return red beans to saucepan and add beet sugar. Cook over low heat, stirring constantly for about 5 minutes. Add salt and mix well. Remove from heat and spread paste on a tray to cool.

7. Unmould jelly by dipping the jelly moulds into hot water. Invert onto serving plates and serve immediately with red bean paste on the side.

The creamy, nutty flavour of the red bean paste complements the slight bitterness of the green tea jelly. This dessert will not satiate or tire the palate.

almond & walnut caramel cookies

Makes 16 bar cookies

Sliced and blanched almonds 50 g

Walnuts 50 g

Wholemeal flour 75 g, sifted

Unbleached plain (all-purpose) flour
75 g, sifted

Aluminium-free baking powder a pinch,
sifted

Ground almonds 20 g, sifted

Maple syrup 30 g

Sea salt a pinch

Vanilla extract 1 tsp

Safflower or grapeseed oil 70 g

CARAMEL

Brown rice syrup 80 g

Maple syrup 40 g

Safflower or grapeseed oil 40 g

1. Without preheating oven, toast the almonds and walnuts at 150°C for 20 minutes. Leave to cool, then chop walnuts into small pieces. Set aside.

2. Increase oven temperature to 160°C. Sift flours, baking powder and ground almonds together twice.

3. Combine maple syrup, salt, vanilla and oil in a bowl and mix well. Add flour mixture and fold in using a spatula. Rub dough quickly with your fingers until crumbly.

4. Sandwich dough with parchment paper and roll it out to a thickness of about 5 mm. Peel off top layer of paper. Place a 18 x 18-cm square cake ring on the dough to shape it. Trim off any excess dough from the sides.

5. Transfer dough with cake ring and parchment paper onto a baking tray. Prick dough all over with a fork. Bake for about 25 minutes, then remove from heat and leave to cool on a wire rack. Increase oven temperature to 170°C.

6. Make caramel. Combine brown rice syrup, maple syrup and oil into a small saucepan and bring to a boil. Cook mixture until thickened, then add walnuts and almonds and mix well. Pour caramel over baked cookie sheet and smooth evenly with a scraper. Return to the oven and bake for another 20 minutes or until golden brown.

7. Remove cookie from heat and leave to cool on a wire rack. When cooled, cut into 16 square bars. Store in an airtight container at room temperature for up to 10 days.

apple brownies

Makes one 18-cm cake

Rum 2 Tbsp

Instant coffee granules 6 g

Unsweetened baking chocolate 30 g

Olive oil 60 g, or substitute with safflower
or grapeseed oil

Unbleached plain (all-purpose) flour
150 g

Cocoa powder 30 g

Aluminium-free baking powder 1 tsp

Maple syrup 150 g

Brown rice syrup 50 g

Ground almonds 50 g

APPLE MIXTURE

Green apples 2, cored and evenly sliced

Maple syrup 3 Tbsp

Lemon juice 1 Tbsp

Raisins 40 g

1. Preheat oven to 170°C. Lightly grease an 18 x 18-cm square cake pan with a little olive oil.

2. Prepare apple mixture. Combine all ingredients in a small saucepan and cook until apples are caramelised. Lay apples on a tray and leave to cool.

3. Combine rum and coffee together in a small bowl and mix well.

4. Melt chocolate over a pot of simmering water. Mix in olive oil and stir to combine.

5. Sift flour, cocoa powder and baking powder together twice. Set aside.

6. Combine rum and coffee mixture, maple syrup, brown rice syrup and melted chocolate mixture in a bowl and whisk together. Add flour mixture and ground almonds. Fold in with a spatula. Add apple mixture and mix well.

7. Pour mixture into prepared cake pan and smoothen with a scraper. Bake for 30 minutes until cake springs back when touched.

8. Remove cake from heat and leave to cool on a wire rack. Slice to serve. If storing, wrap with cling film and store in the freezer for up to 2 weeks.

fig & apricot tart

Makes one 20-cm tart

Dried figs 4 pieces

Dried apricots 7 pieces

Apricot jam (page 148) 100 g, but replace castor (superfine) sugar with beet sugar

TART SHELL

Wholemeal spelt flour 75 g

Unbleached plain (all-purpose) flour 75 g

Aluminium-free baking powder a pinch

Maple syrup 30 g

Sea salt a pinch

Vanilla extract 1 tsp

Soy milk 1 tsp

Safflower or grapeseed oil 60 g

ALMOND CREAM

Unbleached plain (all-purpose) flour 40 g

Aluminium-free baking powder 1/2 tsp

Ground almonds 70 g

Ground hazelnuts 50 g

Maple syrup 50 g

Agave syrup 50 g

Soy milk 50 g

Safflower or grapeseed oil 40 g

Vanilla extract 1 tsp

1. Bring a saucepan of water to a boil. Poach figs and apricots, then drain and pat dry with paper towels. Chop into small pieces and set aside.

2. Make apricot jam (page 148), but castor sugar with beet sugar. Weigh out 100 g jam and store remaining jam for other uses.

3. Preheat oven to 180°C.

4. Make tart shell. Sift flours and baking powder together twice. Combine maple syrup, sea salt, vanilla, soy milk and oil in a bowl and mix well. Add flour mixture and fold in using a spatula. Rub dough quickly with your fingers until crumbly.

5. Sandwich dough with parchment paper and roll it out to a thickness of 3–5 mm. Place dough over a 20-cm fluted tart tin with a removable base and gently press dough against the sides and bottom edges of the tin without stretching dough. Roll the rolling pin over the top of the tin to trim excess dough. Prick base of tart shell with a fork.

6. Place a sheet of aluminium foil or non-stick baking mat over dough (without covering the edges of the dough), pressing it well into the bottom edges. Place baking weights into tart tin and bake for 10 minutes. Carefully remove weights and aluminium foil when pastry just begins to change colour around the edges. Remove from heat and leave to cool on a wire rack.

7. Keep oven heated at 180°C. Make almond cream. Sift flour and baking powder together.

8. Combine ground almonds, hazelnuts and flour mixture in a bowl and whisk together. Add remaining ingredients and mix well. Fold in poached figs and apricots.

9. Spread apricot jam on base of tart, then pour almond cream over. Use an offset spatula to level cream. Bake tart for about 25 minutes. Remove tart from heat and leave to cool before serving.

chocolate banana tart

Makes one 20-cm tart

Bananas 3

Toasted walnuts for garnish

TART SHELL

Wholemeal spelt flour 75 g

Unbleached plain (all-purpose) flour 75 g

Aluminium-free baking powder a pinch

Maple syrup 30 g

Sea salt a pinch

Vanilla extract 1 tsp

Soy milk 1 tsp

Safflower or grapeseed oil 60 g

CHOCOLATE CREAM

Unsweetened baking chocolate 30 g

Firm bean curd 200 g, drained and pat dry with paper towels

Maple syrup 50 g

Brown rice syrup 50 g

Raspberry purée 40 g

1. Preheat oven to 180°C.

2. Make tart shell. Sift flours and baking powder together twice. Refrigerate for a few minutes.

3. Combine maple syrup, sea salt, vanilla, soy milk and oil in a bowl and mix well. Add chilled flour mixture and fold in using a spatula. Rub dough quickly with your fingers until crumbly.

4. Sandwich dough with parchment paper and roll it out to a thickness of 3–5 mm. Place dough over a 20-cm fluted tart tin with a removable base and gently dough press against the sides and bottom edges of tin without stretching dough. Roll the rolling pin over the top of the tin to trim excess dough. Prick base of tart shell with a fork.

5. Place a sheet of aluminium foil or non-stick baking mat over dough (without covering the edges of the dough), pressing it well into the bottom edges. Place baking weights into tart tin and bake for 20 minutes. Carefully remove weights and aluminium foil when pastry just begins to change colour around the edges, then continue baking until light golden brown for about 10 minutes more. Remove from heat and leave to cool on a wire rack.

6. Make chocolate cream. Place chocolate in a heatproof bowl and melt over a pot of simmering water.

7. Blend bean curd in a food processor until creamy. Add maple syrup, brown rice syrup and raspberry purée and mix well. Mix in melted chocolate.

8. Peel, then slice bananas. Spread half of chocolate cream onto base of tart, then top with an even layer of banana slices. Spread remaining chocolate cream over bananas, then arrange any remaining banana slices on top of cream.

9. Garnish tart with toasted walnuts, then place in the refrigerator to chill lightly before serving.

chestnut & miso cake

Makes one 17-cm cake or 7 cupcakes

Unbleached plain (all-purpose) flour
130 g

Aluminium-free baking powder 1 Tbsp

Beet sugar 80 g

Soy bean paste (miso) 40 g

Sticky Chinese yam 100 g, grated

Water 90 g

Safflower or grapeseed oil 30 g

Store-bought steamed chestnuts
100 g, cut into halves

1. Lightly grease a 17-cm round cake pan with a little oil, or if making cupcakes, line 7 round tartlet tins with paper muffin cases. Sift flour and baking powder together. Set aside.

2. Combine beet sugar and soy bean paste in a bowl and mix well. Add yam and beat to combine. Add water and oil and mix well. Add flour mixture and fold in with a spatula. Fold in chestnut halves.

3. Pour batter into prepared cake pan or tartlet tins. Heat water in a steamer until boiling, then steam over high heat for about 20 minutes or until cake is well-risen. Remove from steamer and leave to cool on a wire rack.

4. Serve warm or at room temperature.

Refrigerate cake or cupcakes if not serving immediately. The soy bean paste used in the batter tends to cause the cake or cupcakes to spoil easily in warm weather.

strawberry & red bean rice flour balls

Makes 4 balls

Red bean paste (page 170) 160 g

Glutinous rice flour 70 g

Water 110 g

Potato flour for coating

Small strawberries 4, washed and hulled

1. Make red bean paste (page 170). Measure out 160 g red bean paste and set aside.

2. Mix glutinous rice flour with water in a microwave-safe bowl. Cook in a microwave oven at 600w (Medium) for 1 minute. Stir well, then return to the microwave oven and cook for another 1 minute.

3. Remove dough from bowl and coat with potato flour to prevent it from sticking. Divide dough into 4 even portions and roll each portion into a ball. Set aside.

4. Measure out 4 portions of red bean paste, each about 40 g. Roll into balls, then flatten slightly. Place a strawberry on each portion and roll red bean paste up to enclose strawberry.

5. Flatten a ball of dough and place a red bean ball in the middle. Use your fingers to gently stretch the dough to enclose red bean ball. Repeat with remaining portions.

6. Dust rice flour balls lightly with potato flour to prevent them from sticking. Serve immediately.

bonus recipes for pets

chicken liver cookies

Makes about 40 big cookies or 80 small cookies

Chicken livers 200 g

Soy milk 80 g

Egg 1

Wholemeal bread flour 100 g

Cornmeal 100 g

1. Preheat oven to 150°C.

2. Without oil, stir-fry chicken livers until dry. Transfer to a food processor and blend well. Add soy milk and egg and blend well. Add flour and cornmeal and mix until a dough is formed.

3. Place dough on a floured surface and knead lightly. Roll out to a thickness of about 5 mm. Cut out as many cookies as possible using cookie cutters of choice.

4. Place cookies on baking trays lined with parchment paper. Bake each batch for about 30 minutes until cookies are dry and crisp. Remove from heat and leave to cool on a wire rack.

5. Cookies can be stored in an airtight container at room temperature for up to 10 days or in the refrigerator or freezer for up to 2 months.

bonito cookies

Makes about 40 big pieces or 80 small pieces

Wholemeal bread flour 100 g

Unbleached plain (all-purpose) flour 50 g

Cornmeal 100 g

Bonito flakes 50 g

Egg 1

Soy milk 130 g

1. Preheat oven to 150°C.

2. Combine flours, cornmeal and bonito flakes into a food processor and blend well. Add egg and soy milk and blend until a dough is formed.

3. Place dough on a floured surface and knead lightly. Roll out to a thickness of about 5 mm. Cut out as many cookies as possible using cookie cutters of choice.

4. Place cookies on baking trays lined with parchment paper. Bake each batch for about 30 minutes until cookies are dry and crisp. Remove from heat and leave to cool on a wire rack.

5. Cookies can be stored in an airtight container at room temperature for up to 10 days or in the refrigerator or freezer for up to 2 months.

homemade jerky

Makes about 100–150 g jerky

Chicken breast 200 g

Chicken gizzards 100 g

1. Preheat oven to 120°C. Line a baking tray with parchment paper.

2. Place chicken in the freezer for a few minutes to make it easier to slice, then slice into 5-cm long pieces. Place chicken pieces on prepared baking tray.

3. Make small cuts in gizzards without cutting all the way through. Open gizzards up so they lie flat. Place gizzards on prepared baking tray with chicken.

4. Bake for about 1 hour until chicken and gizzards are completely dry. Remove from heat and leave to cool on a wire rack.

5. Store in an airtight container in the refrigerator for up to 2 weeks or for up to 2 months in the freezer.

Jerky is unbelievably simple to make at home and you can be sure that what you make does not contain preservatives and chemicals!

birthday cake for pets

Makes one 15-cm cake

CARROT AND SPINACH SPONGE

Wholemeal flour 30 g

Unbleached plain (all-purpose) flour 50 g

Eggs 2

Maple syrup 25 g

Carrot 70 g, coarsely grated

Spinach 30 g, boiled, drained and minced

SOY CREAM

Sugar-free apple juice 100 g

Agar-agar powder 1 tsp

Firm bean curd 200 g, drained and pat dry with paper towels

CAROB CREAM

Carob powder 2 Tbsp

Water or apple juice 2 tsp

1. Preheat oven to 170°C. Prepare a 15-cm round cake pan with a removable base. Line with parchment paper. Sift flours together.

2. Lightly beat eggs with a whisk. Add maple syrup and beat with an electric mixer on high speed until eggs are fluffy. Reduce speed and mix lightly for about 1 minute. Gently fold in flours, carrot and spinach with a spatula.

3. Pour batter into prepared cake pan and bake for 25 minutes. When cake is done, unmould from cake pan and place in a big plastic bag to cool.

4. Make soy cream. Combine apple juice and agar-agar powder in a small saucepan and heat gently until agar-agar is completely dissolved. Blend bean curd in a food processor, then add apple juice mixture and blend thoroughly.

5. Make carob cream. Measure out 100 g soy cream and mix with carob powder and water or apple juice.

6. Spread remaining soy cream over cooled sponge cake evenly with an offset spatula. Spoon carob cream into a piping bag fitted with a 1-cm piping tip and decorate cake as desired.

sweet potato balls

Makes about 30 balls

Japanese sweet potato 100 g, scrubbed clean

Soy bean powder (*kinako*) 1 Tbsp

Black sesame seeds 1 Tbsp, toasted and ground

Rice flour 3 Tbsp

Soy milk 3 Tbsp

1. Cut sweet potato into small pieces. Place in a microwave-safe bowl and cover with cling film. Cook in a microwave oven at 600w (Medium) for 2 minutes or until potato is tender and cooked through.

2. Transfer cooked sweet potato to a food processor and pulse into small pieces. Add remaining ingredients and blend until a dough is formed.

3. Roll dough into a ball and knead it lightly on a floured surface. Divide dough into 30 even portions and shape into balls.

4. Bring a pot of water to a boil. Add sweet potato balls to cook in batches until they float to the surface. Remove and drain well.

5. Preheat oven to 160°C. Place balls on a baking tray lined with parchment paper and bake for 10 minutes. Remove from heat and leave to cool on a wire rack.

6. Store sweet potato balls in an airtight container in the refrigerator for up to 1 week or in the freezer for up to 1 month.

weights and measures

Quantities for this book are given in Metric, Imperial and American (spoon) measures. Standard spoon and cup measurements used are: 1 tsp = 5 ml, 1 Tbsp = 15 ml, 1 cup = 250 ml. All measures are level unless otherwise stated.

LIQUID AND VOLUME MEASURES

Metric	Imperial	American
5 ml	$\frac{1}{6}$ fl oz	1 teaspoon
10 ml	$\frac{1}{3}$ fl oz	1 dessertspoon
15 ml	$\frac{1}{2}$ fl oz	1 tablespoon
60 ml	2 fl oz	$\frac{1}{4}$ cup (4 tablespoons)
85 ml	$2\frac{1}{2}$ fl oz	$\frac{1}{3}$ cup
90 ml	3 fl oz	$\frac{3}{8}$ cup (6 tablespoons)
125 ml	4 fl oz	$\frac{1}{2}$ cup
180 ml	6 fl oz	$\frac{3}{4}$ cup
250 ml	8 fl oz	1 cup
300 ml	10 fl oz ($\frac{1}{2}$ pint)	$1\frac{1}{4}$ cups
375 ml	12 fl oz	$1\frac{1}{2}$ cups
435 ml	14 fl oz	$1\frac{3}{4}$ cups
500 ml	16 fl oz	2 cups
625 ml	20 fl oz (1 pint)	$2\frac{1}{2}$ cups
750 ml	24 fl oz ($1\frac{1}{5}$ pints)	3 cups
1 litre	32 fl oz ($1\frac{3}{5}$ pints)	4 cups
1.25 litres	40 fl oz (2 pints)	5 cups
1.5 litres	48 fl oz ($2\frac{2}{5}$ pints)	6 cups
2.5 litres	80 fl oz (4 pints)	10 cups

DRY MEASURES

Metric	Imperial
30 grams	1 ounce
45 grams	$1\frac{1}{2}$ ounces
55 grams	2 ounces
70 grams	$2\frac{1}{2}$ ounces
85 grams	3 ounces
100 grams	$3\frac{1}{2}$ ounces
110 grams	4 ounces
125 grams	$4\frac{1}{2}$ ounces
140 grams	5 ounces
280 grams	10 ounces
450 grams	16 ounces (1 pound)
500 grams	1 pound, $1\frac{1}{2}$ ounces
700 grams	$1\frac{1}{2}$ pounds
800 grams	$1\frac{1}{2}$ pounds
1 kilogram	2 pounds, 3 ounces
1.5 kilograms	3 pounds, $4\frac{1}{2}$ ounces
2 kilograms	4 pounds, 6 ounces

OVEN TEMPERATURE

	°C	°F	Gas Regulo
Very slow	120	250	1
Slow	150	300	2
Moderately slow	160	325	3
Moderate	180	350	4
Moderately hot	190/200	370/400	5/6
Hot	210/220	410/440	6/7
Very hot	230	450	8
Super hot	250/290	475/550	9/10

LENGTH

Metric	Imperial
0.5 cm	$\frac{1}{4}$ inch
1 cm	$\frac{1}{2}$ inch
1.5 cm	$\frac{3}{4}$ inch
2.5 cm	1 inch